Enlightened Contemporaries

Enlightened Contemporaries

Francis, Dōgen, & Rūmī

Three Great Mystics of the Thirteenth
Century and Why They Matter Today

STEVE KANJI RUHL

Monkfish Book Publishing Company
Rhinebeck, New York

Enlightened Contemporaries: Francis, Dōgen, and Rūmī: Three Great Mystics of the Thirteenth Century and Why They Matter Today © 2020 by Steve Kanji Ruhl

Paperback ISBN 978-1-948626-13-2
eBook ISBN 978-1-948626-13-2

Library of Congress Cataloging-in-Publication Data

Names: Kanji Ruhl, Steve, author.
Title: Enlightened contemporaries : Francis, Dōgen, & Rūmī : three great
   mystics of the thirteenth century and why they matter today / Steve
   Kanji Ruhl.
Description: Rhinebeck, New York : Monkfish Book Publishing Company, 2020.
   | Includes bibliographical references.
Identifiers: LCCN 2020000401 (print) | LCCN 2020000402 (ebook) | ISBN
   9781948626132 (paperback) | ISBN 9781948626149 (ebook)
Subjects: LCSH: Mysticism--Comparative studies. | Spiritual
   life--Comparative studies. | Mystics--Biography. | Francis, of Assisi,
   Saint, 1182-1226. | Dōgen, 1200-1253. | Jalāl al-Dīn Rūmī, Maulana,
   1207-1273.
Classification: LCC BL625 .K35 2020 (print) | LCC BL625 (ebook) | DDC
   204/.220922--dc23
LC record available at https://lccn.loc.gov/2020000401
LC ebook record available at https://lccn.loc.gov/2020000402

Book and cover design by Colin Rolfe
Cover background image by Erland Ekseth

Monkfish Book Publishing Company
22 East Market Street, Suite 304
Rhinebeck, NY 12572
(845) 876-4861
monkfishpublishing.com

Contents

Introduction: Three Mystics for Our Time   vii

Chapter One: Who They Were: Francis, Dōgen,
and Rūmī in Their Thirteenth-Century World   I

Chapter Two: Speaking to Us Across Centuries   59
    Love 59
    Nature 68
    The Body 76
    The Role of Women 81
    Spiritual Retreat and Social Engagement 87

Chapter Three: The Poetic Works: A Brief
Comparative Survey   93

Chapter Four: What Francis, Dōgen, and Rūmī
Offer Spiritual Seekers Today   109

Appendix: Some Further Considerations
Regarding Mysticism   139

Notes   145
Bibliography   157
Acknowledgments   167

Introduction

Three Mystics for Our Time

"All mystics speak the same language,
for they come from the same country."
Louis Claude de Saint-Martin[1]

A Christian: bearded vagabond, barefoot, gaunt and frail in his ragamuffin tunic of sackcloth. He roves the hills of northern Italy. He sings God's praises to the skylarks, to roses and the wild cypress.

A Buddhist: abbot in black robes, his head shaved. Seated cross-legged in hushed recesses of a temple in the mountains of Japan, he dabs inkbrush to paper, composing verses as a wisp of moon emerges over pine forests and snow.

A Muslim: scholar with lavish whiskers, his head enwrapped in a turban. He saunters in silk robes through markets of a city in Turkey, past the domed mosques, chants echoing from porticoes of the *madrasahs*. Exploring merchant stalls of lustreware and carob, apricots and lemons he improvises poems of delight, his rhapsodies to Allah, to the Beloved.

*　*　*

They vanished from the earth more than 750 years ago, yet these three spiritual teachers—Francis of Assisi, the Christian saint; Dōgen Kigen, founder of Sōtō Zen Buddhism in Japan; Jalāl ad-Dīn Muhammad Rūmī, the Islamic Sufi teacher—inspire us.

Here is Francis: "This great charismatic and Christlike figure of utter humility and simplicity created a new spiritual consciousness in the Christian West," writes one scholar. "His sense of God's all-pervading presence, his intensive love for all God's creatures, great and small, human and animal, gave the Church an important spiritual legacy that has attracted fresh attention again and again, not least…in our own time."[2]

And Dōgen: He is "now regarded internationally as an outstanding philosopher, mystic, and poet," a recent author notes. "In modern days, his work has had a tremendous impact, not only in Japan…but in the West as well, where he's been discovered by philosophers, scholars, and Buddhist practitioners." Another writer mentions Dōgen's "rise to stardom" and adds, "Dōgen must be by now our most famous Zen master."[3]

And Rūmī? "In the Islamic world today," according to one of his biographers, "Rūmī is read for much the same reasons he was revered during his life: for his excellence as a poet; for his rare ability to empathize with humans, animals and plants; for his personal refinement; and, above all else, for his flawless moral center and ability to direct others towards good conduct and union with Allah." In the West, admiration for Rūmī's work also has blossomed; recently he ranked as one of the best-selling poets in America.[4]

Remarkably, these spiritual teachers lived in the same era. Though they never knew each other, their lifetimes overlapped in the first half of the thirteenth century. Christianity, Buddhism, and Islam differ tremendously, yet Francis and Dōgen and Rūmī, through undertaking the mystical path to quiet the "small self" of ego, were transformed by experiences that help to connect, at the source, all religions. The Christian saint would have described his experiences in terms of receiving fully the grace of God's presence. The Zen Buddhist would have described his as awakenings to original Buddha-nature. The Muslim Sufi would have described his as subsistence in Allah, the Beloved. Because Francis, Dōgen, and Rūmī lived these transformative experiences so profoundly, we truly may call them enlightened contemporaries.

Yet what accounts for the enduring popularity of this long-dead Christian, this medieval Zen monk and this Islamic Sufi spiritual master?

First, each grappled with theological and social issues that continue to reverberate in our own time, and they did so—like many people today—by searching for meaningful experience outside the orthodox confines of church, temple, or mosque. Francis, Dōgen, and Rūmī confronted questions related to the natural world, or to the role of women in society, or to the spiritual dimensions of love, and in doing so they reached beyond the religious dogmas of their era and devised innovative responses that can excite and inspire modern readers. For instance, Francis arrived at a revolutionary understanding of the ecological relationship between humans and animals and the green, living world, an understanding profoundly relevant to our environmental crises today. Dōgen welcomed women fully as equals, with a fervor and conviction that leaps from the thirteenth century directly into the twenty-first. Rūmī created a vivid means of infusing celebrations of erotic longing and passion with an ecstatic yearning for God, linking earthly love metaphorically with heavenly Paradise, and doing so in a way that speaks compellingly to men and women in our current times.

Second, Francis, Dōgen, and Rūmī—in a medieval era when the average person seldom ventured far from home—became unusually well-traveled, embarking on journeys that vastly expanded the range of their understanding, in ways that feel modern to us, cosmopolitan, and enduringly relevant. Francis roamed Italy, walked into France and Spain, and sailed to Egypt. Dōgen left Japan and trekked throughout southern China. Rūmī wandered far from his birthplace in present-day Afghanistan, into lands now known as Iraq and Syria and Arabia to settle finally in the region known today as Turkey. Each of these spiritual seekers, venturing on his personal odyssey, found new means to broaden his world. We identify with that.

Third, each founded a significant spiritual order that still flourishes, seven-and-a-half centuries later. Francis, seeking a radical new path within the Roman Catholic Church, began the Franciscan Order and saw it grow dramatically within his lifetime, from a dozen friars near Assisi in northern Italy to an organization of thousands spread throughout Europe and, soon after his death, into Asia. Today, Pope Francis bears his name. Dōgen, also a spiritual pioneer rebelling against the religious establishment, started the school of Sōtō Zen as a means of purifying Buddhism; with headquarters in Japan, the Sōtō sect now claims adherents worldwide and thrives with particular vigor in America. Rūmī, going beyond conventions of orthodox Islam, founded the Mevlevi order of Sufis, those "whirling dervishes" who today draw enthusiastic crowds to their international appearances. In founding their own orders, Francis, Dōgen, and Rūmī revitalized the religious traditions they loved, which—from their viewpoints—had become rigid and lifeless. They sparked those traditions with fresh energy and authenticity.

Fourth, each created enduring works of poetry. These mystical poets also pioneered writing in the vernacular. Francis's poem "The Canticle of Brother Sun" became one of the first works written in everyday Italian, at a time when European authors composed in high Latin. Dōgen, fluent in the lofty Chinese favored by learned aristocrats in medieval Japan, nevertheless chose to write many of his poems in the Japanese idiom of his countrymen. (And his mighty philosophical masterwork the *Shōbōgenzō*, written in prose, became the first major work written in common Japanese.) Rūmī's *Mathnawī*, an enormous collection of verses, forsakes elevated Persian literary traditions for ordinary speech, raptly extolling the Divine in imagery from everyday life.[5]

Fifth, each responded to tumultuous violence and uncertainty in his lifetime. During an era not only of breathtaking cultural advancement and technological change, but of invasions, acts of terror, bloody conflict, and religious corruption, each one responded by turning inward. They did not become hermits. They remained actively engaged with others. But as mystics, seeking a rigorous yet joyously direct path of sacred experience, Francis, Dōgen, and Rūmī demonstrated with uncommon clarity and zeal the virtue of the inner way, often turning aside from a chaotic, discordant world to a realm of prayer or meditation to seek spiritual harmony. Many of us yearn today for such inner peace.

Sixth, and perhaps most important, these spiritual masters remain popular because they teach us that we can change our lives. Francis had been a wine-tippling playboy; Dōgen, a restive and disillusioned wanderer, near despair as he sought fulfillment; Rūmī, a humdrum, conventional lawyer. Each opened to an experience that transformed his life. Francis heard the startling voice of Christ in an abandoned Italian chapel. Dōgen, sitting countless hours of meditation in a Chinese monastery, suddenly burst into a flash of enlightened clarity, "casting-off body and mind." Rūmī encountered a Sufi holy man named Shams-i-Tabrīzī and swooned in ecstatic realization that here before him stood the very mirror of the Divine Beloved. Such experiences profoundly reshaped the three men, as if recoding their DNA. As a result, each could offer his existence as a living example to his followers, demonstrating daily the possibilities of knowing God intimately through Jesus Christ, or realizing one's innate Buddha-hood, or entering blissfully into the unveiled presence of Allah.

Every one of us can achieve what Francis, Dōgen, and Rūmī accomplished. Though gifted with sensitivity and brilliance, they did not possess supernatural powers. Born as ordinary mortals, they persevered through years of disgruntlement and confusion. Their grit and harsh devotion, their grinding discipline, their aspiration, their fierce refusal to quit made them exceptional. Yet each of us can summon those qualities. Francis, Dōgen, and Rūmī labored toward inner transformation until, finally, they rediscovered their shared human birthright, one we all hold in common—the capacity for mystical experience, for unmediated contact with the sacredness of the cosmos.

Their societies did not teach this. Social values instructed people of the privileged classes to seek power and riches and fleeting pleasures. Francis, son of a wealthy merchant, could have done so. So, too, could Dōgen, born into one of the most aristocratic families in Japan. So could Rūmī, scion of a distinguished scholar. But Francis, Dōgen, and Rūmī urge us to seek spiritual riches. In the Christian mysticism of Francis, union with God is known as Illumination, the *unio mystica*; in the Zen Buddhism of Dōgen, realization of Original Nature is called *satori*; in Rūmī's Islamic Sufism, extinction of self is *fanā* and the perdurable abiding in Allah is *baqā'*.

Of course these three mystics were not the first to seek such experiences. Many other followers of Jesus or Buddha or Mohammed had done so for centuries—as had Hindu devotees of Shakti or Krishna, or Jewish mystics faithful to God and the secrets of Torah.

Like these mystics, Francis, Dōgen, and Rūmī show people on the spiritual path how to set aside the "small self" of ego to experience a sacred conjunction of the worldly and the eternal. Because they describe the path so vividly, and because their own lives serve as powerful examples for seeking the path with unflagging ardor and commitment, they help make the way of enlightenment accessible

not only to their fellow Christians, Buddhists, or Muslims, but to all
of us.

*   *   *

People often look askance at the word "mysticism." To some it suggests the realm of the preposterous, the hopelessly obscure. To others
it hints merely at hocus-pocus and harmless chicanery, at parlor games
both spooky and silly: candles and incense and Ouija boards. To some,
"mysticism" means fuzzy thinking. And to still others—often within
the mystic's larger, more orthodox faith community—the word con-
notes the weirdly aberrant, the vaguely sinister, the wild-eyed ravers
locked in religion's closet.

In fact, however, mystical experience lies at the most profound
depths of our spiritual consciousness. It glows as a powerful light at
the core of all religions. Its remarkable process neutralizes the "small
self"; it expunges the petty ego, the "I am," with its incessant blather
of "me, me, me," narcissistic and deluded. In doing so, it liberates
a spiritual seeker to find both the miracle of the specific here-and-
now and the miracle of the Infinite. As the sense of personal isolation
dissolves, the mystic awakens to a deep rapport with all of life. This
sense of communion awakens, too, a heart awash in love. How does
such an awakened life manifest in the world? Judging by the evidence
of Francis, Dōgen, and Rūmī, it manifests as a life tempered by suffering, yet pulsing with energy, with meaning, with spiritual gravitas
balanced by lightness and agility, with compassion, with clarity of
presence, with sagacity, and with fearless joy.

It is necessary to demystify mysticism.

Mystical experience can happen to anyone. It can happen to
you. In fact, it should. It needs to, regularly, if you expect a sane,
wholly functioning life. The ability to directly experience the sacred
comes as part of our human birthright, as part of our natural sensory

equipment. Our brains, our ears and eyes, our skin, our cells have all the necessary receptors. Our spirits take nourishment from regular mystical experiences—from holding "Infinity in the palm of your hand /and Eternity in an hour" as William Blake put it[6] —just as our physical bodies take nourishment from food. Mystical experience is normal and healthy. Every single one of us can have mystical experiences; in fact, *we are meant to have them*. We can learn the requisite openness and attentiveness. Nothing but our distraction and busyness, our harried, jumbled minds, our dulled senses, our obsessive multi-tasking and our gadgets and our frantic diversions prevent us each day from seeing the Absolute in the mundane, from seeing the sacred in the ordinary—from glimpsing paradise, on a July morning, within a purple aster. As William Wordsworth lamented, "Getting and spending, we lay waste our powers." [7] Yet we can touch Eternity at any instant. Like Francis, like Dōgen, like Rūmī, we simply need to reach out our hand.

The powerful sense of "awakening" or "grace" common to mystical experiences can be triggered by widely diverse events. Again, the fundamental criterion is a direct experience of the Absolute without the mediation of a centralized ego. It is a transport beyond the self. This can happen in numerous ways. Mystical experiences may occur in moments of placid calmness, or in orgasmic bliss; they may occur among daily chores such as sweeping the floor or in moments of initially terrifying—even life-threatening—emergency, as in combat. They may occur during a vision quest, or a shamanic journey initiated by a divine psychotropic plant, or during an uncanny dream. Mystical experiences may occur during prolonged ceremonies of ritual dancing and drumming, as in the ecstatic Sufi *sama* known to Rūmī; or during a sustained period of prayer, fasting, and contemplation, as in the Christian hermitage known to Francis; or in rigorous days and nights of continual meditation, as in the Zen *sesshin* known to Dōgen. They also can occur sitting in a traffic jam and glancing at a sunset. In that transformative instant, petty "me-centered" vexations and concerns may drop away into an experience of still presence. It feels like a sudden gift.

The mysticism of Francis, Dōgen, and Rūmī was grounded thoroughly, as we shall see, within their historical contexts of thirteenth-century Christian northern Italy (then part of the Holy Roman Empire), Buddhist and Shintō Japan, and Islamic Ṣūfī society in Turkey (then known as central Anatolia, a Persian culture ruled by the Mongol empire). Yet, despite their unique historical determinants, the mystical experiences of Francis, Dōgen, Rūmī, and others share universal commonalities. This is why a person who knows mystical experience firsthand, who is tuned to that wavelength, can instantly recognize similar experience described by someone from another era and another culture. It is why such a person in twenty-first century America can explore Francis, Dōgen, or Rūmī—or Lao-Tse or Hildegard or Shantideva or Black Elk—and say, "Yes. I recognize this. Much of the intrinsic core of this is familiar to me, even if the terminology and symbols differ. I've experienced something very close to what they describe. I know the reality they're pointing toward. These people are my companions."

(A more detailed discussion of mysticism follows in Chapter Four and in the Appendix.)

How did they accomplish it? And how do they guide spiritual seekers today?

Before we can begin to explore these questions, we must acquaint ourselves with the outstanding lives of Francis and Dōgen and Rūmī, and with the wondrous era that formed them.

Chapter One

Who They Were:
Francis, Dōgen, and Rūmī
in Their Thirteenth-Century World

In 1200, a wealthy nineteen-year-old carouser and spendthrift dwells in the lively hillside town of Assisi in a north central Italian province of the Holy Roman Empire. Giovanni di Pietro di Bernardone, rechristened as "Francesco" by his father, belongs to one of the prosperous families in Italy's emerging middle class of traders and merchants. The elder di Bernardone deals in sumptuous furs, bolts of colored fabric, Chinese silks. The son, Francesco—or "Francis"—an affable youth, loves to romp through ancient Roman streets of Assisi by torchlight with rowdy friends. Skimpily educated by monks, with a smattering of elementary Latin, some basic arithmetic on the abacus, and a bit of Bible recitation, Francis as a young boy tramped to merchant fairs in the Champagne region of France with his father, and there under banners and tents the proud tradesman groomed him to master the family business. By the year 1200, however, Francis shows little interest. Wenching, guzzling wine, shouting bawdy songs, he shows off his splendid clothes and hosts lavish parties. Rollicking companions proclaim Francis "Master of the Revels."

In 1200 skirmishes ravage the Umbrian region of Italy. Two years earlier, a grisly war erupted over tensions between traditional landed nobles and Assisi's rising merchant class. The nobles and their knights had allied themselves with the pope. Merchants of Assisi massacred them on the battlefield and burned their castle. Francis, loyal to his merchant family, had forsaken wine and revels long enough to help his clansmen haul logs and stones, building ramparts and fortifications around Assisi. Now, the danger temporarily abated, he devotes himself again to merry-making.[1]

Dōgen's life commences at the very daybreak of the thirteenth century. His birth into Japan's aristocracy occurs at the imperial capital of Heian-kyō in January of 1200. We know the city today as Kyoto.

The medieval Japan of Dōgen's lifetime is a country of feudal estates and illustrious riverside cities. On the estates, warlords rule from stone castles or from manor houses protected by log palisades and moats, guarded by lancers on horseback. Archers and gruff swordsmen, from bellicose clans of the samurai, live inside those walled compounds. Outside the gates lie fields green with rice. Peasants hoe the fields near thatched huts. In outlying monasteries, bounded by cedar forests and mountains, robed Tendai Buddhist monks, summoned by temple bells, chant the Lotus Sutra in candle glow and incense.

The cities of Dōgen's Japan boast market plazas and cobbled thoroughfares. Splendid with pagodas and sequestered gardens, with teahouses and carved bridges in miniature plum orchards, with Buddhist temples lavishly gilded and Shinto shrines of bright vermilion, these commercial centers—Heian-kyō, Kamakura, Osaka, Edo— jostle with guild artisans and merchants. Sailboats dock at wharves for unloading. Silk importers, rice brokers, fishmongers, raucous traders of salt and seaweed and charcoal ply the streets and alleys, shoving handcarts. Vendors stack live chickens in bamboo cages. Dealers shout prices for lacquerware. Shop owners haggle for Chinese porcelains or sandalwood sticks, herbal medicines, plush brocades. They clamor amid woodsmoke, in straw-matted rooms open to the avenues.

Descended from the tenth-century Emperor Murakami, Dōgen is born in Kyoto's royal enclaves, probably to a woman named Ishi, daughter of a famed warrior and poet in the mighty Fujiwara clan. His father most likely is an elderly, high-ranking member of the illustrious Minamoto family named Michichiku (also spelled "Michichika" or "Michitomo" in some sources), a "well-known sensualist" and poet who serves at court as Lord Keeper of the Privy Seal. Dōgen's birth is tainted by scandal. As calculated by the arcane and inflexible social standards of the imperial court, his mother lost prestige when earlier in life she married a disgraced general then later deserted him. As a result, when she remarried, to the eminent Minamoto, her new husband outranked her so greatly that their socially awkward marriage has failed to receive the sanction of court officials. At the birth of their son, Dōgen, those officials declare the newborn an illegitimate child.[2]

Nevertheless Dōgen enjoys a pampered boyhood near the grounds of the palace. At the age of two, his father dies, but his mother and his oldest half-brother—another Minamoto, who brushes poems in delicate calligraphy and serves as a minister of state—raise the child in tasteful refinement among his elder sisters and brothers. Many of them have risen to eminence at court. At the age of four Dōgen begins to study classical Chinese and Japanese literature, a typical education for a son of the nobility.[3] The boy also sees robed Buddhist priests scurrying through hallways from the royal temples, intent on their religious duties to the emperor and his family. The young Dōgen is clad in perfumed raiment of silk, befitting a young lord. He moves in whispers through his mother's quarters, through lamplit rooms of his tutors in the imperial compound.

The fourteenth-century Japanese classic *Confessions of Lady Nijō*, the autobiography of an imperial courtesan in Kyoto, suggests the lushness of daily life Dōgen witnesses as a growing child. In that rarefied realm within the walls of the palace compound, amid ponds of golden *koi* and gardens of chrysanthemum and sculpted pine, elegant men and women, each a lavishly costumed dilettante, engage in indolent banquets and *sake* parties, murmur gossip, dabble at poetry, and indulge in ceaseless romantic intrigues amid the rustle of silk kimonos.

As strife continues in Italy, in the winter of 1202 Francis takes up his sword. Bankrolled by his father, the young gadabout gaily dons a knight's helmet and chain-mail armor. Mounting a charger he trots with merchants of Assisi to war with neighboring Perugia, across the Tiber River, stronghold of the surviving aristocrats. This time, however, the nobles exact revenge. Their troops, wielding maces and battle-axes, arrows and halberds, slaughter men of Assisi on the open plain. Francis falls wounded. Taken prisoner, he languishes for a year in a foul dungeon. When ransomed by his father the scrawny Francis burns with malaria. He spends the next year bedridden, attempting to recover. In 1205, when he dons his armor and helmet and again mounts the saddle to join a military expedition, he grows sick on the first day. Faint, he receives a dream vision. A voice urges him to return home. Francis, the dream voice tells him, needs to await his true calling.[4]

* * *

Political clashes rip across thirteenth-century Japan as well. The emperor, an effete figurehead, holds court in Kyoto, surrounded by ladies in waiting and perfumed dandies. There he engages in state ceremonies, plum-wine parties, poetry, and moon-viewing among the cherry blossoms. Meanwhile the regent and his shōgun, official leaders of the country, rule from the palace of Kamakura with their military governors. Battalions of bowmen, regiments of fearsome cavalry in leather and armor, and troops of dogged foot soldiers provide the regent's armed strength. He struggles to maintain the allegiance of rival warlords throughout the countryside. The warlords govern domains from hulking castles of hewn stone, assisted by samurai who pledge their swords and their lives. Conflict often explodes between these various political factions, revolts followed by bloody reprisals. Sometimes militant fighter-monks called *sōhei* from provincial Buddhist monasteries join the samurai in combat.

On the nobles' feudal estates, straw-hatted peasants who grub through years of exhausting toil in rice fields find solace in religion. Some practice a synthesis of Shintōism—with its reverence for nature spirits and its fear of demons—and Pure Land Buddhism, a new Japanese sect founded by Hōnen and elaborated by Shinran, elder contemporaries of the young Dōgen. The sect appeals to ordinary, unlettered people. It offers salvation to those who entrust themselves to the Vow of Amida Buddha. This simple promise holds vast appeal, especially in 1257 when an earthquake will topple cities in the Kamakura region, and two years later when corpses of thousands of people felled by famine and plague will litter avenues of Kyoto. The promise of the Pure Land also entices people in those years when anarchy seems imminent, as truculent Buddhist monks armed with swords and spears march into Kyoto and brawl with swordsmen in muddy streets and courtyards mired with blood. Many thirteenth-century Japanese believe they live in an "Age of Degenerate Law," an era when Buddhist teachings have irremediably decayed.[5]

Often they complain that monasteries of the Tendai sect and of Shingon—an esoteric, tantric Buddhism—have become wealthy, lethargic institutions, showplaces of magnificent gardens and gold-leafed temples, lorded over by bureaucratic priests in silken finery and costly purple robes. Aristocratic patrons finance these temples to ensure their own spiritual comfort. In Kamakura they help pay for construction of the bronze Daibutsu, the Great Buddha statue. By the late thirteenth century a firebrand named Nichiren, born in 1223, will start his own breakaway sect of Buddhism, a movement zealously nationalistic, angrily demanding reform, and devoted to the scripture of the Lotus Sutra.

One of the most significant developments in Japanese religion during the thirteenth century, however, will become the importing of a subversive, stripped-down, ferociously uncompromising form of Buddhism from China called Ch'an. Though focused on silent meditation, Ch'an also features a zesty, iconoclastic spirit. Brought to Japan by Eisai, who has introduced a type of Ch'an meditation that emphasizes grappling with riddles called *kōans* to burst through delusions into sudden enlightenment, he will be followed by Dōgen himself, who as an adult will become a passionate reformer. Dōgen will employ *kōans* as training tools, but his Ch'an practice will stress sole reliance on the liberating power of meditation. Ch'an Buddhism will become renowned in Japan as "Zen."

While Japan remains locked in feudalism, the thirteenth-century kingdoms known to Francis are starting to emerge from it. Europe is bustling. A new cash-driven economy is developing. In the kingdom of France, in the Holy Roman Empire, in the kingdom of England, people clear beech forests and sow wheat and rye and barley to feed a growing population—75 million by century's end. Windmills churn on hillsides. Dirt lanes and cobbled roads, long disused, now throng with pilgrims, students, minstrels, and traveling merchants, who sojourn in hostels, inns, or Benedictine monasteries.[6]

The roads connect medieval towns. Outer walls of these towns enclose gabled houses, high-steepled churches, huts roofed with thatch. Dim, narrow lanes meander between tenements sooty with wood smoke. They stink of garbage slops and raw sewage. Public squares of the towns swarm with honking geese, with tradesmen in doublets of dark blue or leggings of scarlet, with itinerant musicians hoisting lutes and tambours. They move among tonsured monks, scavenger dogs, lank-haired children and lame beggars dragging on crutches, among pickpockets, among leaping jugglers in feathered caps. Gangs of soldiers, pikes slung over their arms, shove past rooting pigs. Aproned housewives at the butchers' stalls examine fly-specked rabbits or plucked hens for purchase. The towns host markets and fairs. In the countryside, lords maintain vast manors. They rent acreage to tenant farmers, who work grain fields and live in mud-daub shacks roofed with straw. Dukes and princes build extravagant stone castles on commanding plateaus, replete with turrets and battlements, where, on the parade grounds, retinues of mounted knights joust and rehearse for the next Crusade, cantering in tunics beneath heraldic banners, under scrutiny of ladies to whom they pledge chivalric loyalty.

Cities flourish in the Europe of Francis: Venice, Paris, London, Frankfurt, Toledo. Though mere towns by Asian standards, and filthy, nevertheless they boast in the 1200s a spectacular surge of architectural innovation, as the spires of newly built Gothic cathedrals loft heavenward. Arched buttresses allow the cathedrals' massive bulk of stone to float effortlessly in air—buoyant apparitions of pastel-tinted glass and radiant light. Europeans dedicate many of their new cathedrals to Our Lady, as veneration of the Virgin Mary, which began to spread in the mid-1100s, continues through the thirteenth century.

In naves of those cathedrals, under shimmering rose windows, wealthy aficionados in Francis's era can gaze upon gilt reliquaries, frescoes of Biblical tales, or sacred paintings, flat and in Byzantine style, of the Madonna and Child. They can savor, in private chambers of lavishly endowed monasteries, troves of illuminated manuscripts, psalters, and bestiaries shimmering with gold. In halls of castles they can admire tapestries of winsome ladies and kneeling unicorns and lions. They can enjoy the sculpted stone figure of a regal woman at Naumburg Cathedral, striking in her verisimilitude, or the more stylized realism of figures at Reims Cathedral in France or, in the German realms, those at Strasbourg Cathedral or Bamberg Cathedral, with their gracile limbs and flowing robes. Giotto observes similar statues in Italy and studies them thoroughly, learning to give solidity and volume and life to his painted figures. Born in 1266, by the end of the century Giotto will start an artistic career that will make him one of the great virtuosi of Western painting. Among Giotto's most esteemed work, dating from 1290, will be the cycle of murals he creates to honor the life of Francis.[7]

At a time when Buddhist monasteries in Dōgen's Japan have succumbed to extravagant wealth and corruption, the Christian Church in Europe also has grown bureaucracy-ridden, doctrinaire, and torporous with pomp and riches. "Many priests have lived luxuriously," writes one of the popes, Innocent III. "They have passed the time in drunken revels, neglecting religious rites. When they have been at Mass, they have chatted about commercial affairs....They have made a scandalous commerce of relics."[8] Meanwhile the popes themselves bask in palatial luxury in Rome. They rule a papal state that vies with kings for worldly power. They summon armies to enforce their dictates and they threaten recalcitrant princes with excommunication—which to people in the High Middle Ages means the terrifying certainty of infinite eons scorching in hell.

The Church does rouse itself to send armed Crusaders against Muslims in the Middle East. In 1204 the venture gets sidetracked and Crusaders gut, instead, the Eastern Orthodox Christian capital of Constantinople, looting it then raping and massacring the inhabitants. The Church interrupts its Crusades and recruits troops in 1208 to burn alive the French people known as Cathars and in 1209 to slaughter those called Albigensians, who are Gnostic rebels against Christian orthodoxy living within the Provençal homeland of Francis's mother. In 1217, Crusaders set out under their banners of the Holy Cross, get mired in the marshes of northern Egypt during the bloody siege of Damietta, finally win against the Muslims, then are thwarted by the flooding Nile as they try to win Cairo. The Church also launches an Inquisition throughout Europe in 1232 and, again in the name of Jesus, roasts heretics alive in public bonfires. In 1248 Crusaders will return to Egypt in hopes of killing more Muslims in the name of Christ; they suffer yet another defeat.[9]

Amid this carnage, cities in Francis's thirteenth-century Europe witness a glorious pre-Renaissance of learning, much of it derived from the torrent of Greek and Arab knowledge emerging from conquered cities of Islamic Spain. They rush to build prestigious universities: Florence in 1221; Naples in 1224, the first to be completely free of Church control; Toulouse in 1229; the Sorbonne in Paris in 1253; Cambridge in London later in the century.

Within drafty and dim lecture halls of these universities a new interest in science and philosophy burgeons. People of all classes and levels of education in Francis's lifetime, and in the decades immediately following, believe in witches, sorcery, angels, horned demons, hellfire and celestial paradise. Yet science—or "natural philosophy"— begins to develop in Europe later in the century, with the work of Roger Bacon, who will send bound copies of his handwritten books *Opus maius* and *Opus minus* to the pope in 1267. Influenced by the Islamic scholar Avicenna's translations of Aristotle—whose natural philosophy Bacon teaches at colleges in Paris and Oxford—and by the Islamic scholar Alhazen's publications on optics, Bacon (who will become a member of the lay Order founded by Francis) nevertheless insists that knowledge derived only from books is deficient. He argues robustly for a "science of experience." He demands testing through induction and experiment. In this he resembles another proto-scientist of the age, Albertus Magnus.[10]

Mathematics, too, advances in Europe during the lifetime of Francis. Immensely influential, the book *Liber abaci* helps spread the knowledge of Arab mathematicians and the use of Indian-Arabic numerals throughout Europe. It appears in 1202, penned by Leonardo Fibonacci, a brilliant Italian mathematician well-known for his elegant "Fibonacci Sequence," who also makes contributions in solving cubic equations.[11]

Rational philosophy reaches milestones in the Europe of the thirteenth century as well. Thomas Aquinas, born in Italy in 1225 (the year Francis of Assisi will die), composes his monumental works *Summa contra Gentiles* and *Summa Theologiae* to reconcile Roman Catholic theology with the reasoning of Aristotle, seeking rational proofs for the existence of God. Appearing in 1264 and 1268, in later centuries they will form the cornerstone of the Church's scholastic philosophy.[12]

Francis, with little patience for logical disputation, prefers song and poetry. In his medieval world, troubadours in the French Provençal and minnesingers in the German lands create for Western Europe a fresh lyrical form, singing elegant verses in praise of courtly love. Following the example of the eleventh century "Song of Roland" in France, scribes during the 1200s for the first time write down traditional folk stories, derived from oral ballads, and circulate them as epic national literature: "El Cid" in the Spanish kingdoms, the tales of King Arthur in England, the Nibelungenlied in the German fiefdoms, the Icelandic sagas.[13] Later in the century Dante Alighieri will emerge. Born in Florence in 1265, by century's end Dante will compose his masterful sonnet sequence, the heartfelt *La vita nuova*.

Cultural triumphs throughout Europe are accomplished against political upheavals of wars and the intrigues of kings. French troops rain volleys of arrows against hapless knights of English, German, and Flemish battalions on the fields of Bouvines, and their victory in 1214 helps crown France as the premier kingdom of Europe. For much of the century the prayerful Louis IX, later canonized as Saint Louis, rules from his throne in Paris. English nobles force their autocratic King John, vanquished at Bouvines, to resentfully affix his royal name to the Magna Carta in 1215, bolstering their legal rights. To the east, the sprawling Holy Roman Empire flourishes for thirty years under the rule of Frederick II, the ruthless and flamboyant "Wonder of the World," an outstanding scholar, linguist, and arts patron who bickers endlessly with the Catholic pontiff, Innocent IV. To the south, high-masted merchant ships laden under heavy sail rove the Mediterranean. Venice shares control of the rich sea routes with Italian cities of the Lombard League. In the far north, the Hanseatic League oversees trade on the snowy Baltic. In that region Teutonic Knights battle pagans in the Baltic Crusades, until Russian horsemen of Alexander Nevsky will trap the Knights on a frigid day in 1242, and destroy them on a frozen lake.[14]

*   *   *

Francis had hoped that he, too, would become a knight. But lying sick and half-starving for a year in a dank stone prison in Perugia following his capture in battle shocks and transforms him. There, and while bedridden after his ransom, he questions profoundly the meaning and purpose of his life. Is it all simply carousing and hedonism? Drinking and singing and womanizing and spending his father's money? Dabbling at soldiering? What if he had died out there on that battlefield; what then? What would have been the point of it all? Helpless and pushed beyond despair, he finally surrenders in dazed bewilderment to the only recourse available: to God.

After receiving the dream vision instructing him to await his true calling, in 1207 he wanders the Umbrian countryside feverish with anticipation, his spirit churning, watchful for signs. He prays. Outside the walls of Assisi, in a grove of olives, he enters a ruined chapel called San Damiano. He kneels beneath its sagging roof. Light streams through chinks in the mortar. Francis gazes at a painting of Christ suffering on the cross. As he gazes, he hears a voice. The voice, he believes, emerges from the lips of the stricken Jesus. The Savior says to him, "Francis, don't you see that my house is being destroyed? Go, then, and rebuild it for me."

In that miraculous instant the life of Francis shifts. "Yes, Lord, I will," he answers.[15]

He feels reborn.

In that same year of 1207, across the world in Japan, young Dōgen, a markedly precocious, impressionable child, mourns the death of his mother, a loss he will remember all his life. He will recall standing at her funeral and watching incense smoke drift to the temple ceiling and wondering, in his sorrow, about impermanence and death.[16] Many decades after this loss he will write, in a poem tender with love, "My companions / Trekking / The six realms – / I recognize my father! / There is my mother!"[17] Dōgen will later say that the grievous blow of his mother's death awoke in him the urge to wholeheartedly seek the Dharma, the truth of Buddhist teachings. "Impermanence is a fact before our eyes," he will tell his students when he has grown to become a teacher. "We are born in the morning and die in the evening; the person we saw yesterday is no longer with us today."[18]

Now, however, orphaned at the age of seven, the boy finds himself adopted by a wealthy uncle. The uncle plans a dazzling future for the boy, one designed to initiate him into Japan's ruling class of gentry. Dōgen, it seems, will inherit the life of a dandy at court.

In Italy, shaken by his mystical experience of Christ's voice, Francis at first chooses a hermit's existence. He dwells in the woods and prays. Never one for half-measures, Francis also renounces his wealthy family. During a public hearing at the bishop's court, his scandalized father demands repayment of money from the wayward son. Francis walks forward from the crowd. He stands in the center of the courtyard. "Please listen, everyone. Because I want to serve God from now on, I am giving back to my father the money about which he is so distressed." Then he strips himself naked. "I also give back my clothes." Returning his splendid finery and a purse of gold to his father, Francis proclaims to the stunned onlookers, "In future I will only acknowledge our Father who is in heaven."[19]

Francis now devotes himself to quietly repairing neglected churches near Assisi. Scruffily bearded, dressed in a rough burlap tunic, he puts to good use the skills acquired during wartime when he helped to fortify walls of Assisi; at these local chapels he now fixes broken timbers, plasters walls, cobbles stones. He feels aglow. Each day he prays. He wanders as a beggar, singing troubadour ballads, cheerfully asking villagers for crusts of bread, scraps of turnip, a mug of porridge. He dedicates himself to the Jesus who has spoken to him, and he trusts in God's providence. He sleeps in a cave. And by 1207 he has begun nursing the most wretched outcasts of medieval Italian society—people afflicted with leprosy, universally shunned as vile and horrifying, people officially declared "living dead" by the Church. Francis holds these lepers in his arms. He bathes them. He cleans their festering sores.

On a winter's feast day, listening at Mass to the priest reciting from the Gospel of Matthew, hearing the words of Jesus's instructions to his disciples—roam freely, preaching that the Kingdom of Heaven is at hand; heal the sick; accept no gold or silver; wear but a single tunic and carry no bag and wear no sandals; enter houses and bless them—Francis recognizes his calling. "That is what my whole heart longs to accomplish," he declares.[20]

At first he works alone. Soon, however, the twenty-six-year-old Francis will find himself leading a band of followers. Soon, too, he will meet a young woman who stirs him deeply.

In 1207 as well (year 604 in the Islamic calendar), near the city of Balkh at the far eastern range of the Persian empire, in the land we know today as Afghanistan, Jalāl ad-Dīn—later known as Rūmī—is born.

Balkh, one of the world's most ancient settlements, has enjoyed a long tradition as a colorful international city on the Silk Road, the overland trade route linking the Mediterranean world with central Asia and the fabled riches of China. When Balkh was the capital of Bactria, centuries earlier, it blended ancient Greek, Persian Zoroastrian, and Indian Buddhist cultures, later adding Islam into the mix. Some of the Buddhist notions seem to have lingered in this Afghan city. They may have influenced early Sufi thinking that took hold there. Rūmī's elderly father may be familiar with those Buddhist ideas. A struggling Sufi mystical preacher, legal scholar, and instructor named Mohammed ibn al-Hoseyn Bahā ud-Dīn Walad, he has written the *Ma'ārif (Divine Sciences)*, a treatise on Islamic esoteric spiritual teachings.[21]

Rūmī, like Dōgen but in marked contrast to Francis, thus will grow up in a household that prizes literature and scholarly refinement. When the boy is about three his father moves the family to the nearby city of Samarqand, in present-day Uzbekistan, between the snowcapped mountain turrets of the Hindu Kush and the shores of the Aral Sea.

While Europe has just begun to flourish, the Islamic caliphate far outshines it in cultural flair. Immaculate cities of the Muslims, in lands known today not only as Afghanistan but as Iran, Syria, Iraq, north Africa, and Spain, feature in Rūmī's era libraries and rose gardens, banks and restaurants and hospitals, palm-shaded bath houses and market plazas arrayed among glorious domed mosques and the churches and temples belonging to fellow "people of the Book," the minority sects of Christians and Jews. The young Rūmī's new home of Samarqand is remote from the palace of the caliph in Baghdad. Nevertheless it thrives as one of the many showplace cities of the Islamic world. Like Balkh it is a Silk Road cultural center, resplendent with gilded minarets, with shopping bazaars and camel stalls, book marts and *madrasahs*. Samarqand lies in a fertile valley sheltered from winds that blow across vast plains east of the Caspian Sea, nestled in groves of shade trees near the Oxus River, in the Persian-controlled province of Khorāsān.

But, as in the feudal Japan of Dōgen's youth, and in Francis's northern Italian province of Assisi, vicious strife wracks Khorāsān. In 1212, when Rūmī is barely a five-year-old boy, a clan from a nearby territory besieges Samarqand; their frenzied warriors breach the city's fortress walls then savagely kill hundreds of men and shrieking children and rape and massacre the women. Rūmī's family survives. The boy will never forget the terror of the siege or the slaughter.[22]

Dōgen quits his luxurious home in Kyoto's royal compound during that year of 1212. The aristocratic uncle who adopted him had hoped earnestly that the boy, now a stripling of twelve years old, would don lavish garments to engage in traditional rites marking his public debut into manhood and the august ranks of Japanese nobility. But Dōgen's mother, on her deathbed, had requested otherwise. She wished him to become a Buddhist monk. Dōgen, a pensive youth, still brooding on questions of mortality and transience, honors her wish. Forsaking the city he begins to train at one of the premier Tendai Buddhist study centers, a massive complex called Enryaku-ji, in pagodas secluded atop the forested slope of Mt. Hiei, three thousand feet above the shores of Lake Biwa.[23]

In making his decision, Dōgen emphatically leaves his family and the aristocracy behind. He does so as firmly as Francis did, after publicly returning his clothes and a purse of gold to his father, standing naked before the astonished crowd and before his God.

In the temple Dōgen chants and reads the Lotus Sutra. Years later he will recall the "mystical cry of monkeys / Resounding from the mountain peaks, / Echoing in the valleys below: / The sound of the / Sutra being preached."[24]

Dōgen soon receives ordination in that remote Buddhist monastery. The boy, bundled in his simple brown robes, kneels on tatami mats in a dark hall redolent of agarwood smoke. He bows in *gassho* to his fellow monks. Then he bows to the abbot, head newly shaved.

Francis in 1212—the year Rūmī's family survives the massacre at Samarqand; the year Dōgen leaves home—meets a wealthy eighteen-year-old girl.

This young heiress, spellbound after hearing Francis preach the lessons of Christ, introduces herself. Her name is Clare Offreduccio. She sees standing before her a benign, ebullient tramp. He has a scruff of beard and a bald pate wreathed with hair in a friar's tonsure. He has callused hands like a workingman. He radiates quiet spiritual power, a surety in his mission imbuing him with fervor and authority, an electrifying charisma. He seems to radiate, too, irenic goodness, this man who lives as Jesus did. By now a small band of ragtag devotees follows Francis on his journeys, men inspired by his purpose, his grace, his grinning tenderness, his lilting songs, his simplicity and gentle pauperdom. Hearing him, Clare feels kindled in her blood and in her spirit.

Francis sees standing before him a brown-eyed maiden, slender and comely. Later legends will suggest that she has reawakened his carnal passions. They tell us that to numb his desire he will lie naked in icy puddles and pray. If such passions are arising in him during this first meeting, he commands his soul to subdue them. He sees Clare's purity of spirit. "Peace be with you," Francis says to her.

Soon she, too, vows to follow him. She flees her rich family in Assisi one night. Clare hopes to join Francis's group of vagabonds in a life of poverty, prayer, and service. Francis accommodates her as best he can, within the strictures of the era. He establishes her as a nun, cropping her hair by torchlight. He garbs her in sackcloth. He gives her the chapel at San Damiano—the same chapel among the olives where he experienced his vision of the speaking, crucified Jesus. Word spreads. Other maidens and older, unmarried women and widows soon join Clare to live at the chapel. Declaring obedience to God rather than to husbands and fathers, they feel liberated from some of the constraints imposed on women by medieval society. In a community of women they work quietly together and cultivate a lightness of spirit. They pray. They weed small vegetable gardens, pick and prune the medlar orchards. They weave broadcloth. They nurse the sick. They dedicate their labors to Christ and to Heaven. The Offreduccio girl, later to become Saint Clare, founds the order of Franciscan nuns, which becomes known as the Poor Clares.[25]

Others continue to join Francis. His sense of freedom, his merriment and his mildness combined with his unwavering spiritual sincerity and tremendous drive feel new. It motivates people to transform their lives. Francis has already traveled to Rome, pattering barefoot in his frayed robe through magnificent alcoves of the Vatican palace to meet Pope Innocent and officially gather his followers into an Order, the Friars Minor. The brotherhood consists of wanderers, shoeless and lean in hooded cassocks of dun gray. They emulate Francis, praying as they feed gruel to people moaning from fevers. In an age when Bibles and other books are rare, and most people are illiterate and could not have read them anyway, these men purvey a simple message that speaks to the heart. They trek into village squares and, instead of screaming about sin and hellfire like the local priests, speak of kindness and love. "Peace be with you," they murmur, smiling. They speak not in elegant Latin of the church officials but in the rough-hewn Umbrian dialect of the common people. Like Francis, they trade their labors each day for scraps of rye crusts, sleeping at night in stone huts. Sometimes people mock them or pelt them with garbage. Most, however, rejoice.[26]

When a friar asks why so many flock after him, Francis replies, "You want to know why after me? You really want to know why everyone is running after me?" It is because God has seen that no one is "more vile or insufficient than I am," Francis says. "In order to do that wonderful work which He intends to do, He did not find on earth a viler creature, and therefore he chose me, for God has chosen the foolish things of the world to put to shame the wise, and God has chosen the base things of the world and the despised, to bring to naught the noble and great and strong, so that all excellence in virtue may be from God."[27]

As Dōgen later will, Francis chooses to live in the wild. He favors a small, out-of-the-way chapel of Santa Maria near Assisi in land known as the Portiuncula, a shaded, low-lying terrain where brooks and marshes open in dense forests of ilex and oak. From there he often hikes in dawn mists up to a hermitage on the wooded slopes of Mount Subasio, nested in a high ravine near cliffs and caves. Francis preaches God's love to ravens, to wild hares, to butterflies and foxes.[28]

Francis soon decides to hike the pilgrims' route into Spain. For weeks he and his new companions journey until they cross rocky passes of the southern Alps. They march over the coastal plain of France. Then through foothills of the Pyrenees. They sleep under clouds and stars. Sometimes they walk alone; often they walk among other devout travelers. Roving by day on dirt roads and sheep paths they brave hunger and sudden storms and armed brigands. After months of hiking Francis arrives in the Spanish kingdoms of Navarre and Aragon. That torrid land of brilliant light nurtured the Islamic culture of Andalusia. Now Christian knights have conquered it, and Francis travels among the restored churches, the fortress towns with their fragrant vineyards, the groves of olives and Seville oranges, the hillside castles. En route to the popular Christian pilgrimage site of Santiago de Compostela he cares, as always, for the sick. He praises and pets fondly the yoked oxen and the dray horses, the cattle and the ragged goats, and he sings to God.

The journey aggravates his ill health. But it inspires him to expand his Order of friars into the Spanish kingdoms. During the next seven years he also witnesses the expansion of his loosely organized group of five thousand mendicant brothers into France, the German realms, and England. Additionally, his Third Order of laypeople—men and women who take vows similar to the friars' but who remain in village life—continues to grow.[29]

Returning to his native Italian provinces in the Holy Roman Empire, to the wooded hills he loves, Francis continues to bequeath himself fervently to God, in the *vita apostolica* of poverty, chastity, and obedience, subsisting in heartfelt and authentic imitation of Jesus. He instructs people through the model of his life.

Often Francis, beaming happily, humming his favorite Provençal tunes, wanders into Umbrian towns to preach. In an era of vicious bloodshed, he greets crowds with words to assuage their yearning: "God give you peace." He and his friars urge people to offer good works and do penance and forgive others. Sometimes while telling stories of Jesus, Francis cheerfully sings impromptu concerts for people gathered around market stalls in village squares, prances for giggling children, or clowns and pantomimes and plays the fiddle. Other times Francis hides in seclusion. He starves in prolonged fasts. He prays alone, days reeling into long nights. He braves raw, dark regions of the human psyche where few dare to venture. He weeps in empathy with the tortured Christ. He emerges into light, his spirit renewed.

According to biographies of Francis that will be written soon after his death by Friar Thomas of Celano, the "little saint of Assisi" also feels uncommon affection for wild creatures, and intimacy with them. He preaches to doves and jackdaws. He speaks to "Sister Swallows" as they chatter and make nests. He frees "Brother Rabbit" from its snare. He throws captured fish back into the water. He befriends "Brother Pheasant" and "Sister Cricket." He pacifies a wolf that has terrified villagers, bidding it to live gently.

He never becomes a priest. He loves "Holy Mother Church" and reveres the daily sacred miracle of the Eucharist, and urges his friars to respect clergy and pope. He observes the daily Hours, from Matins to Vespers and Complice, in hymns and prayer. He observes, too, the Church calendar of feast days and fast days. Yet Francis always refuses to ordain. He chooses instead to live as Jesus did. In every aspect of his life he offers rebuke to his beloved Church of Rome, a church that

Francis sees clearly has bloated itself with gold and become heartless and pompous and cruel.

Given a choice between listening to the Church and listening to God, Francis listens to God.[30]

In about 1219 Rūmī, now twelve years old, joins his family and his father's disciples as they flee the war-scarred region of Khorāsān. Rūmī's family desperately hopes to escape the approaching Mongol army.

*　　*　　*

The Mongols dominate much of the world in the 1200s, and their ruler, Chinggis Khan, alters it dramatically. His mounted archers, with their severe, wind-burned faces and drooping mustaches, wear quilted tunics with rawhide cuirasses and they ride stocky horses bred for endurance on the open steppes. In battle each of these archers can empty a quiver of arrows at full gallop. Renowned for their unyielding ferocity, they have thundered out of the central Asian grasslands. Half the realms of earth, from China to Europe, quail before the onslaught. The Mongols incite an age of terror.

Chinggis Khan is establishing the vastest land empire in history. Like Mohammed five hundred years earlier, who united for the first time bickering desert tribes of war-loving Bedouin nomads—and like Mohammed's successors, who then sent those horsemen storming out of the Arabian peninsula to seize every kingdom in their path—so Chinggis Khan has united belligerent tribes of Mongol nomads from the arid northern steppes and unleashed them against the world.

The Mongol ruler is more than a bold and canny military tactician, however. He proves a remarkably able administrator. And, like Francis and Dōgen and Rūmī, he devotes himself to his religion. But it differs from anything his three contemporaries would recognize. It involves venerating ancestors, and praying to an image of an earth goddess, and revering the potent spirits of wind and fire and running water; above all, it honors the supreme god known as Mongke Koko Tengri, or Eternal Blue Sky. This mighty deity controls the invisible spirits, both benign and evil, thought to influence life on the plains of northern Asia. Mongols believe that Chinggis Khan himself lives as the earthly representative of Eternal Blue Sky, entrusted with a divine mission to conquer the earth. Anyone who resists Chinggis Khan defies the will of God.

Thus Chinggis Khan feels justified, in his holy mission, to pillage and massacre towns that resist his horsemen. Rūmī's family barely escapes one such massacre, when he is a boy and the Mongols strike the recalcitrant city of Samarqand—seven years after the city's destruction by the Khwarezmians—and butcher everyone they find. Rūmī's father leads his clan westward, ahead of the Mongol invasion. They are fortunate. Throughout Asia, Chinggis Khan's marauders torture, rape, and murder en masse those who offer defiance, raze their cities, kill their animals, then on the charred rubble stack towering pyramids of human skulls.

But Chinggis Khan and his dynastic successors also allow kingdoms that surrender peacefully to retain their social and religious customs, whether Christian, Buddhist, or Muslim, as long as they accept Mongol rule and pay generous tribute in gold, silver, horses, silks, and furs.[31]

*   *   *

At twelve years old, Rūmī and his family, their small caravan of pack donkeys loaded with carpetbags, trek arduously westward toward present-day Iraq. About 1220 they sojourn in Baghdad, a city—three decades before its destruction by the Mongols—of half-a-million people.

It is easy to imagine their experience, based on historical accounts of the capital:

They glimpse reed huts in the marshes. Boats on the languid waters of the Euphrates and Tigris. Among interlacing canals they see mud-brick houses and whitewashed terraces and, beyond, shining in the sun, the imposing walls and gilt domes of the caliph's palace. Throughout the city they hear the strident singsong of the *muezzins* alerting people to pray. Winding through Baghdad's labyrinthine alleys the young Rūmī and his family see men gossiping among marble columns of arcades, or playing chess, and veiled women splashing water into jugs at wells in the mosque courtyards. Passing through crowded streets among buildings of glazed brick, of stucco and glass, buildings with arched windows, arabesque friezes and inlaid mosaics of blue lapis and gold, they arrive in a hubbub of market plazas, where slaves lead camels or cool their masters with palm fans, and where bearded shopkeepers in turbans weigh coins on scales or rush into banks to cash checks—a Muslim innovation—penned in Arabic. In the bazaars of Baghdad people eat roasted lamb spiced with coriander and cumin, examine porcelain vases and bolts of silk from China, compare prices of tethered falcons, peruse Scandinavian armor and the carved ivory casques from Timbuktu, capital of the black Islamic kingdom of Mali. Near these markets the young Rūmī sees men chattering in taverns, sipping mild raisin wine and listening to strummed zithers. He sees one of Baghdad's many hospitals or pharmacies, or its public bath houses, or its paper mills. He strolls with his father in a garden of pavilions and burbling fountains, among lilies and caged nightingales. On steps of libraries he overhears students debating Ibn Rushd's commentaries on Aristotle. Throughout each day he sees men in Baghdad's mosque sanctuaries, near the *quibla* wall, bowing toward Mecca on prayer carpets.[32]

Many decades later he will remember that city, in his poems of the *Mathnawī*, as a place of sacred magic and power: "In the spirit you are a prince // for whom Baghdad and Samarqand are half a step away. Animal / energy lights your eyes // and quickens your step. Your hair grows and shines with / that energy, but move into // the deeper energy that derives from. There Muhammad / will welcome you, and // Gabriel will back away saying, 'If I came closer, your / glory would consume me.'"[33]

Leaving Baghdad, Rūmī's family embarks on a sacred pilgrimage. They hike hundreds of miles south. After months of walking from village to village and traipsing the caravan paths and camping in open country they reach broad sand flats and heat-shimmering Arabian dunes of the Bedouin tribesmen. Then they walk for days toward mountains of the Red Sea. They enter Mecca. In that gleaming desert city they join thousands of other Muslim pilgrims who cleanse themselves, don white garments, and kiss the Black Stone of the *Kaaba*. After days of ritual and prayer at the holy shrines Rūmī's father leads the entourage northward through the sand wastes again on a long, footsore trek into Syria, sojourning in the learned capital of Damascus and perhaps also in Aleppo and in other cities. Finally they reach central Anatolia (present-day Turkey), a region known as the sultanate of Rûm. Through his vagabond childhood, Rūmī—the adopted name means simply that he comes from Rûm—will experience transience and uncertainty, but he also comes to know far-flung cultures and diverse social customs of their people, as Francis did, when his father took him as a boy on long journeys from northern Italy to trade fairs among the peddlers and troubadours of France.[34]

In the year of the young Rūmī's departure from Afghanistan, 1219, Francis experiences for the first time the salt breeze and vast blue expanse of the Mediterranean as he sails its roiling waves to Egypt. He has shipped out with swordsmen and archers who have painted crosses on their helmets and shields. These soldiers have joined the Fifth Crusade, and Francis accompanies their "glorious" quest—as he initially thinks of it—to rescue God's sacred city of Jerusalem from the "infidels" of "unholy" Islam. Francis hopes to convert Muslims to faith in Jesus or else die as a martyr. After landfall on the Egyptian coast, he marches with Crusader troops to the Muslims' besieged fortress city of Damietta. There, in the hot, squalid, disease-ridden Christian camps outside the city's walls and towers, Francis discovers wounded men, wailing in their filthy bandages. He sees the sick ones wet with heat and delirium. Crusaders swill wine, toss dice in gambling games, loll in their tents with whores. Many, devoted not to God but to pelf and plunder, bicker over loot.

Shocked, Francis finds the commander of Christian forces. Receiving permission to venture past dunes and broken palm groves of the no-man's land, he walks directly into the Muslim lines. Francis hopes to meet with the Ayyubid sultan, al-Malik al-Kamil, and end the warfare. Islamic chronicles will later record that when startled Muslim sentries see this beatific little hobo striding toward them, he reminds them of a Sufi holy man. They allow him to pass unharmed.

Beneath canopies of the Muslims' royal tents, reclining on silk cushions and layered medallion rugs amid hanging tapestries, watched by Saracens with their headscarves and their curved swords, Francis finds a polite welcome from the learned, debonair, and deeply pious al-Kamil. They meet throughout the week, speaking through interpreters. Francis speaks of Christ with his customary ardor, and the sultan, revering Jesus as a great prophet in the Qur'an, listens attentively and explains the teachings of Mohammed. Perhaps Francis and al-Kamil pray together to God, beseeching Him for a merciful end to the war. At any rate, Francis emerges from these meetings with a newly awakened respect for those he once considered demonic.

The sultan grants him permission to make a pilgrimage out of Egypt to the Holy Land. Thus Francis might journey to Bethlehem at Christmastime, though neither Thomas of Celano nor Bonaventure mention it later. Perhaps he walks to the battle-scarred Jerusalem. If so, he probably kneels and prays at the Tomb of the Holy Sepulchre and views, across the rubbled streets, the Muslims' golden Dome of the Rock. Or, enfeebled by disease and malnourishment and chronic fatigue, perhaps he forsakes the journey and simply rests in Egypt for the voyage home.[35]

On his return to northern Italy in 1220, Francis finds his Order riven by dissent. Many of his friars demand a way of life resembling the more established Christian orders, such as the Benedictines and Cistercians. Weary of dozing on moss and leaves, of begging for scraps, of wandering, they want to own beds and chairs in houses with cozy hearths. They want to study theology in universities. They want a charter of formal monastic rules. Francis, in poor health, coughing and wheezing at thirty-eight, reluctantly drafts such rules. The pope approves them. Francis then shows what he thinks of these developments: the barefoot man who owns nothing and wanders freely, who calls himself a "fool for God," singing to his "brothers" and "sisters" mouse and bee, hare and partridge, blessing each hawthorn and briar rose, greeting each person he meets with the smiling benediction of "God's peace be present here," informs his friars, "Henceforth I am dead to you." Francis permanently resigns as head of the Franciscan Order.[36]

While Francis struggles and Rūmī and his family roam throughout the medieval Middle East, Dōgen in 1223 arrives in Song Dynasty China.

Since shaving his head and ordaining with the robe and bowl of a Tendai Buddhist monk a decade earlier, he had distinguished himself as a relentless and unusually gifted student, one who asked probing questions. Dōgen's most persistent and troubling query: if all human beings are endowed from birth with Buddha-nature, why must we struggle so hard to achieve enlightenment? The question nipped and harried him. In his spiritual struggle Dōgen sat on *tatami* mats in candlelit rooms and queried the Tendai priests. Their answers failed to satisfy him.

At the age of fourteen, then, he had forsaken the Tendai school on its mountaintop overlooking Kyoto and discovered in the city a new temple founded by Eisai, an elderly teacher who had brought to Japan the rigorous Chinese Buddhism called Lin-Chi Ch'an—or, in

Japanese, "Rinzai Zen." As a Tendai monk, Dōgen had grown adept in study of the Lotus Sutra, steeping himself in its parable of the three carriages and the burning house, its tale of the *nāga* princess, its prophecies, its miracles and pronouncements. In Eisai's eclectic mix of Rinzai Zen and other Buddhist forms, though, Dōgen found his first taste of radical practice. He studied with Eisai, seated for hours on a black cushion in meditation, fixated on the oral tradition of rid-dle-like *kōans*: "A monk asked Tung-shan, 'What is Buddha?' Tung-shan said, 'Three pounds of flax,'" or "Wu-tsu said, 'It is like a buffalo that passes through a latticed window. Its head, horns, and four legs all pass through. Why can't its tail pass through as well?'" or "The priest Pa-chiao said to the assembly, 'If you have a staff, I will give you a staff. If you have no staff, I will take a staff from you.'"

(Chinese *kong-an*, rendered in Japanese as "*kōans*," though several centuries old and transmitted by word of mouth prior to Dōgen's era, were appearing in newly printed compilations when he began to study them. The collection of *kōans* called the *Hekigan Roku*, or *Blue Cliff Record*, was compiled in China during the twelfth century; according to legend Dōgen may have introduced it to Japan. The *Mumon-Kan*, or *Gateless Gate*, collection of *kōans* as well as the *Shōyō-roku, or Book of Equanimity*, collection of *kōans* and commentaries both were com-piled during Dōgen's lifetime.)

The old teacher Eisai soon died. Dōgen, adrift, sought another spiritual teacher. He tried each temple—wood and plaster behemoths with massive sloping roofs, their sliding paper screens opened to reveal alcoves guarded by bodhisattva statues and, within, vast worship halls of smoking altars and golden buddhas. He wandered Kyoto for three years. He sat in halls pungent with incense and listened to talks on *sutra* passages and abstruse points of dharma. No priest inspired him.

Restless, Dōgen went back to the Rinzai Zen temple and began to study with Eisai's highest-ranked disciple, Myōzen. A warm rela-tionship developed. Attired in black robe and brown *reihaku*, Dōgen trained intently, honing his concentration, deepening the placid *samadhi* state of his meditation, glimpsing bright, exhilarating moments of clarity each time he hammered his way through a new *kōan*. Yet he had not resolved his question: if enlightened from birth, why such struggle for enlightenment?[37]

Now, by 1223, Dōgen feels discouraged by conventional Buddhism, not only in Kyoto but throughout the small, sequestered islands of Japan. He chooses to sail with his teacher Myōzen by masted ship to the great kingdom across the sea. The journey takes two months. "Through a voyage of countless miles," he will write, "entrusting my transient body to the billowing waves, I finally reached Great Song" Dynasty China.[38] There, he knows, Buddhism has long flourished.

While docked in the Chinese seaport of Ningbo he meets an old cook visiting from a Ch'an monastery, whose conversation quickens and challenges him. "Good man from a foreign country," the cook tells Dōgen, "you do not yet understand practice or know the meaning of the words of ancient masters." Do not understand practice? Dōgen probably wonders at this. He has been a monk for more than ten years. Do not understand words of the masters?

When they meet again, Dōgen refers to this shipboard conversation and asks, "What are words?" The cook answers, "One, two, three, four, five." Dōgen asks, "What is practice?" The cook replies, "Nothing in the entire universe is hidden."[39] Later Dōgen will recount this meeting with the gnarled and wily Ch'an cook in 1223 as one of the decisive events in his quest. For the next two years Dōgen, now in his early twenties, anxiously seeks his path to enlightenment. He roams from temple to temple in southern China.

*　　*　　*

During the 1200s the China of the Southern Song Dynasty claims 100 million people, describes itself as the Center of the Earth, believes its emperor ordained by Heaven, and views everyone beyond its realms as a barbarian. It has ample reason. When Marco Polo arrives near the end of the century, China will astound him. The refinement of its civilization exceeds anything the European has imagined.

In fiefdoms of Italy and France, Germany and England, a book remains a luxurious rarity, painstakingly hand-copied by monkish scribes; in China, educated people amass personal libraries: volumes of poetry, Neo-Confucian treatises, or illustrated catalogs of apricot and plum, all printed using the medieval high-tech innovation of moveable woodblock type, a Chinese invention in widespread use two centuries before Gutenberg.

Paddle-wheel boats, sixty feet long, chug along China's rivers. Boats transporting tons of millet and wheat from fertile fields in outlying districts unload at vast mills; there water-powered wheels spin gears turning grindstones that crush the grain to flour. Wooden barges carry rice from newly terraced paddies south of the Yangtze. Other boats ferry ore to coke-fired blast furnaces; thirteenth-century China produces twice as much iron as England will at the start of the West's Industrial Revolution, six hundred years from now, and China has already been doing so for two centuries. Use of coal as fuel remains unknown in medieval Europe, but the Chinese burn it routinely (Marco Polo will gaze in awe at fires kindled from "black stones"). They use gunpowder, also unfamiliar to Europeans. Moreover, Chinese sailors from the coastal city of Quanzhou and the great southern ports set out to sea in gigantic triple-masted junks. These state-of-the-art sailing ships feature such marvels as multiple decks, stern-post rudders, and watertight partitioned hulls. China's mammoth vessels, large as a modern department store, float a thousand men each, venture to the Indian Ocean, and their skippers navigate by watching the needle of a magnetic compass, yet another Chinese invention.

China during the 1200s continues to export coveted, mass-produced trade goods to international markets. Splendorous brocades and cut silks, crackle-glaze stoneware, and the prized, bluish-white *qingbai* porcelain vases are shipped hundreds of miles westward to the Islamic world and, through the Mediterranean ports, to Europe, on routes traveled by Chinese merchandise since the era of the Roman empire. In return China receives treasure from kingdoms spanning half the globe.

Wealth from this trade supports not only China's booming population of workers and merchants and its government network of Confucian scholar-officials, but an aristocracy of learned nobles who patronize a culture of unsurpassed sophistication and artistic virtuosity. Connoisseurs sip from heirloom tea bowls and admire subtle poems brushed by Empress Yang. They linger over album leaves by Ma Yuan. They savor exquisite ink-on-silk paintings of sparrows and crickets among blossoming wisteria, mandarin ducks among iris, swallows among petals of crabapple. They murmur appreciation for handscrolls of dragons in swirling clouds, or northern landscapes of cliffs and pines, mists and cataracts. At court they enjoy lavish dance performances and music sparkling with flutes and pipes, harps, drums, and iron chimes.

Chinese cities of the Southern Song—Nanjing, Shanghai, Guangzhou, Ningbo— buzz with traffic. Crowds throng shops and spacious avenues. In 1235, when London is a befouled and dangerous little town of only fifteen thousand inhabitants, the Chinese capital of Hangzhou thrives as a metropolis of more than a million people. A visitor that year will record market plazas bustling from morning till late evening with shoppers. Vendors ply "pearl, jade, talismans, exotic plants and fruits, seasonal catches from the sea, wild game, all the rarities of the world." Similar visitors to Hangzhou see elegant restaurants with hanging lanterns, pawnshops, silk boutiques. They note riverside tea houses near the Grand Canal. Arched "rainbow bridges" lined with peddlers' awnings and parasols. Streets paved with brick and stone. Spring-fed public bath houses, their lavatoriums replete with cold-and-hot water tubs. Government-sponsored health clinics and old-age homes. Spice shops. Wine shops. Market stalls with bins of pears and peaches. Ceramics factories and artisan shops featuring lacquerware and porcelain. Taoist shrines. Confucian academies. Ancient Buddhist temple pagodas. Meeting places for the city's legions of clubs: the West Lake Poetry Club, the Physical Fitness Club, the Young Girls' Chorus, the Antique Collectors' Club, the Plants and Fruits Club. Warehouses. Silkworm factories. Textile mills of racketing looms. Fish markets. Greengrocers. Rice snacks. Archery shops. Three-story inns with broad porches. Fire stations. Travelers on horseback, plump aristocrats carried in sedan chairs, workers pulling wheelbarrows, camel caravans from distant lands arriving on the Silk Road. Monkeys. Magicians. Storytellers. Tax collectors. Barbers shaving customers. Robed merchants with wispy mustaches and goatees. Herbalists. Acupuncturists. Fortune tellers. Women with paper fans, students, soldiers, monks, scholars with kerchiefs, government officials strolling in parks and gardens near the palace gates. And, as proof of unrivaled prosperity, more than a hundred banking establishments in Hangzhou, briskly exchanging not only gold and silver and coins of bronze and copper, but government-issued paper money—the first such currency in the world.

This is the China through which Dōgen travels.[40]

Today, most people in the West think of the medieval era of the 1200s strictly in terms of romance novels or Hollywood. They conjure images of the Middle Ages in England and France: minstrels, knights in armor, princesses in castles. They believe that a populace of lords and ladies, of merchants and serfs and vassals newly emerged from the Dark Ages lived in a culture devoid of further innovation or advances in learning, ruled by overweening kings and popes, until the Renaissance arrived to wake everybody up. Moreover, most Westerners have learned from their school textbooks that the phrase "medieval civilization" refers exclusively to Europe. If we look carefully at the world of Francis, Dōgen, and Rūmī in the thirteenth century, however, we find it much more expansive and much more fascinating than many of us suppose. A global perspective shows that, in addition to China and Japan, the Islamic caliphate, and the Mongol empire, other civilizations existed beyond Europe. Francis, Dōgen, and Rūmī only could have guessed at the scope of these civilizations in their century; some they knew via sketchy information available from caravan merchants and voyagers, and from rumors and tales overheard on their own travels, while the most remote civilizations they did not know at all. But for us to see and understand their world in a broader context is important enough to warrant this brief digression:

During their lifetimes, while Song Dynasty China and its capital of Hangzhou dominate Asia—at least until Mongols overrun it mid-century—another extraordinary realm coexists to the south. The Khmer empire, a Hindu kingdom, stretches from present-day lands of Burma through Cambodia and Laos to Vietnam, and its capital of Angkor near the vast lake of Tonle Sap ranks as the most extensive urban complex in the world, a city sprawling amid cultivated palm and fruit trees for 400 square miles. It consists of palaces, moats, canals, huge reservoirs, rice paddies, storehouses, golden Hindu temples (or, increasingly through the 1200s, Buddhist ones), and the homes—built on stilts, and roofed with woven palm thatch—of more than 750,000 people at the base of the Kulen Hills and headwaters of the Siem Reap River.[41]

Meanwhile, on the other side of the Pacific, in the lands of the Americas, indigenous civilizations are in transition. Farming people called Aztecs are moving into the Valley of Mexico. They migrate following collapse of the brutal, sun-worshipping Toltec empire. These people of the winged serpent and the jaguar settle amid ancient temples of city-states in the Lake Texcoco region. Within a century they will begin their own brutal rise to dominance.

To the east, on warm, fertile plains of the Yucatan peninsula in central America, legions of armed men and boys led by the ruler of Mayapan conquer the venerable city of Chichén Itzá, with its columned Temple of the Warriors and its sacred pyramid of Castillo, in 1221. They establish a line of kings, the dynasty of Cocom.

To the southwest, in green highlands of the Andes near the Pacific coast, people of the mountain forests weave remarkable tapestries bright with patterned motifs of stylized monkeys and leopards; their chieftain Manco Cápac during the period from 1200 to 1230 founds the new kingdom of the Incas, which two centuries later will expand into a mighty South American empire.

Meanwhile, far to the north, among the many elaborate Native American cultures in the present-day United States, the thirteenth century marks the zenith of the Hisatsinom, or Anasazi, and related peoples. Soon they will begin to decline, as they struggle with prolonged drought. But for three hundred years they have built cliff dwellings and vast adobe town complexes, replete with earthen dams, reservoirs, and irrigation systems for cornfields throughout the Chaco Canyon and Mesa Verde region of present-day New Mexico and Colorado. Hundreds of miles of roads, marked by signal stations, connect pueblos that feature multi-story apartments, central ampitheater-plazas, and underground kivas. People trade turquoise deep into Mexico and make baskets and striking geometrically-painted pottery. Women of the Mimbres culture produce exceptional bowls adorned with stunning abstract designs of fish and birds. The era also witnesses, to the east and north, the construction of magnificent temple mounds, steeply terraced pyramids, and cities with expansive avenues and plazas throughout the tribal chiefdoms of the Caddoan people, territories that range the length of the Mississippi River, up to the state we now call Illinois.

Even farther north, Inuits wander through present-day Canada to frozen Greenland in the thirteenth century, where they encounter

Norse settlements, prompting both trading and fighting. Thus the New World meets the Old, though not for the first time; Vikings have been camping on the North American coast for two hundred years.[42]

During this era of Francis, Dōgen, and Rūmī, the black civilizations of Africa are flourishing. The kingdom of Zimbabwe rules mines and trade routes in the continent's southern region, connected to a global network of commerce; Zimbabwe exports gold dust and copper ingots and elephant-tusk ivory, and it imports celadon and porcelain from craftsmen in China, blue-glazed ceramics from artisans in Persia, and fine madras and other cotton textiles from tradesmen in India. The king of Zimbabwe begins in approximately the year 1200 to build the Great Temple near the River Save. A large royal enclosure of shrines, passageways, huts, and a conical tower of stonework within imposing granite walls, it is the most impressive of more than one hundred stone structures throughout this seaside African kingdom, marking the capital of government and serving as a site to worship regal ancestors and the supreme god Mwari.

North of the Congo, in rainforest areas and savannas of Africa's Atlantic coast, the potent black city-state of Ife—ruled by a divine chief overseen by his shamanic priest, devoted to the sky god Olorun—prospers as a hub of lucrative trading networks. There thirteenth-century Yoruba artisans are sculpting in brass and bronze their expressive, superbly rendered portrait busts of black princes and court aristocrats, working masterfully in a realistic mode rivaling contemporary sculpture of Japan and Europe.

North of Ife, bordering the Sahara on the fertile delta of the upper Niger, arises the empire of Mali, a coastal powerhouse in west Africa through the 1200s and into the next two centuries; ruled by black Islamic kings, the wealth of Mali derives from trading gold, ivory, and slaves.

On Africa's eastern coast, in the Ethiopian highlands near the Red

Sea, a small Christian state has survived earlier Muslim invasions into Africa. Here in the thirteenth century King Lalibela directs the building of ten subterranean churches—including the cross-shaped Church of St. George—each hewn from a single freestanding block of volcanic stone within a deeply excavated pit, and each adorned with ornately carved windows, arched vaults, and pillars. Lalibela's underground holy city becomes renowned as the "Jerusalem of Ethiopia." The king, claiming guidance from God, renounces his throne to live as a Christian hermit.[43]

To the north, in Egypt, lies the Islamic sultanate of the Mamluks, ruled by the Turks. Egyptian cities, including Cairo, serve as booming centers for thirteenth-century Sufism. At the crossroads between East and West, Cairo sees as well a large influx of Jewish refugees from the Crusades. In these fertile circumstances, a "pietist movement" emerges in Egypt that effects a blend of Sufism and Judaism. These "Jewish Sufis" choose as their foremost leader, until his death in 1237, the mystical theologian and political leader Abraham Maimonides, son of Moses Maimonides, medieval Judaism's great scholar and rabbi. Abraham Maimonides serves as court physician to Malik al-Kamil—the urbane and religiously tolerant Islamic sultan who met earlier with Francis of Assisi in royal tents at the siege of Damietta during the Fifth Crusade.

Cairo in 1284 also becomes the site of the world's most sophisticated hospital, an Islamic "palace of healing" with unsurpassed medical facilities. It includes a convalescent ward that channels natural spring water to cool the rooms, floors strewn with fragrant herbs to freshen the air, and strolling musicians to comfort patients, who also can listen to men reading the Qur'an. Separate wards treat fevers, surgical cases, and dysentery. This Islamic hospital also comes equipped with laboratories, baths, pharmacies, kitchens, and a lecture theater where doctors give instruction to medical students. Patients receive all treatment free of charge.[44]

One of the things the Turkish Mamluk Sultanate of Egypt does best, however, is wage war. They manage what no one else can do: they halt the southern advance of the Mongols. In 1256 the Mongol horsemen sack and burn the city of Baghdad, thirty years after Rūmī's family has passed through, killing everyone they find. They execute the Islamic caliph by rolling him in a carpet and crushing him with horses. Thus ends the rule of the Abassid dynasty. The Mongols next storm into Syria. The mounted Islamic warrior brigades of the Mamluks in Egypt ride out to meet them. Consisting of former slaves and palace guards of the Abassids, with a well-earned reputation for fury, they stop the Mongols in 1260 during bloody combat at Ayn Jālūt, in deserts near the Sea of Galilee.

Having defeated the Mongols, the Mamluk Sultanate of Egypt in 1291 resolves to do the same to European Christians: its hard-riding Islamic cavalry smashes the Crusader States in Syria and eliminates them once and for all.[45]

For the rest of the thirteenth century, what remains of the enormous Mongol empire reaches from the Pacific shores of Korea to the mountain borders of Poland and Hungary in eastern Europe. It lies under the supreme command of the Great Khan, Kublai. He rules from the conquered China, a prize grabbed by the Mongol horsemen in 1279. He oversees the vastness of Russia, dividing it into the Khanates of the Golden Horde, the White Horde, and the Cheibanid. He oversees the region known today as Iraq and Iran, included in the Persian Khanate, and he oversees the Khanate of Turkestan, where Rūmī dwells.[46]

Marco Polo reaches China during the thirteenth century, in his epic journey that commences in 1271 and lasts through 1295—a trip made possible by those same Mongol horsemen, who have broken the Muslim hold on the Silk Route and opened it again to wayfarers from Europe, exacting tribute from the caravans. By 1296 Christian friars arrive in China to win converts to Christ; the friars, thousands of miles from home, are Franciscans, followers of the little self-pro-claimed "fool for God," Francis of Assisi.

The Mongols in China who greet Marco Polo and welcome the fol-lowers of St. Francis also attempt twice during the thirteenth century to launch a sea invasion of Japan.

In 1274 they land a massive force, consisting of tens of thousands of troops and sailors in hundreds of ships, on the southern Japanese island of Kyūshū. The Mongols use Chinese gunpowder and explod-ing shells fired from bamboo tubes, which the Japanese never have seen before. Outnumbered, local samurai fight the Mongols tena-ciously for two days, suffering heavy losses. Then on the final night a gale arises and destroys the Mongol armada. In 1281 the Mongols invade Japan again. The battle rages inconclusively for fifty days. Then, miraculously, another gale arises. The Japanese know it forever after as the *Kamikaze*, or Divine Wind. It tears the Mongol fleet to splinters.[47]

Continuing to move beyond our standard Eurocentric view of the thirteenth century we see that far to the west of Japan, in India, the foothills of the Himalayas become sanctuary for Muslim refugees of the far-flung caliphate who flee the Mongols, creating a richly hybrid culture. After the Turkish slave-general Quṭb ud-Dīn establishes an Islamic sultanate headquartered in the hot, dusty city of Delhi, for the rest of the century his Muslim successors battle Hindu uprisings, expanding their control from the steamy basin of the Ganges into central India. In the south, however, beyond the forbidding Deccan plains, in the coastal region of teak and sandalwood forests, the Tamil-speaking kingdom of the Chola dynasty continues throughout the 1200s to enjoy its cultural and political golden age as a major Hindu naval and merchant power, trading spices, silks, perfumes, ivory, and gold to other kingdoms across the seas—including the southern Europe of Francis, the Middle Eastern region known to Rūmī, and the China where Dōgen now wanders.[48]

*   *   *

Meanwhile Rūmī, at age seventeen, lives with his family in Larende, a town in Anatolia near the Taurus Mountains with a large Christian population ruled by the tolerant Islamic dynasty of Seljuks. He is beginning a family of his own. Married in 1224 to a young woman named Gowhar Khatun, who had trudged with his clan and others in the long journey from Afghanistan, soon after he fathers two sons. Perhaps after a youth spent in continuous travel, narrowly escaping massacre, he longs for stability and the decorous life of a Muslim householder. Rūmī's spiritual practice, unlike that of Francis's or Dōgen's, takes root in worldly activities of marriage and fatherhood.

Also Rūmī benefits from a first-rate education. In this regard he resembles Dōgen but contrasts markedly with the erratically schooled Francis of Assisi. By 1224 the young Rūmī, brilliant and inquisitive, has been studying throughout the years of journeying with his family, tutored by his father at nightly campfires in Syrian foothills or Arabian palm oases, in tents or quiet gardens during stopovers in Baghdad or Damascus, perhaps in brief interludes at Islamic schools or with a famed teacher in Aleppo. Rūmī has immersed himself in the Qur'an, the legal sciences of the *Shari'ah*, the ancient *Hadith*—reported sayings of the Prophet Muhammad—and lengthy Qur'anic commentaries. He has acquired knowledge in world history. In Muslim theology. In schools of Greek, Indian and Arabic philosophy; in mathematics, including algebra and geometry; in Persian verse writing and prosody; and in astronomical sciences explaining motions of the planets and stars.[49]

In the chill autumn of 1224, while Rūmī tends to his new wife and continues his studies, and while Dōgen travels in China, Francis enters on a spiritual retreat that will affect him profoundly. Three years since his return from Egypt, Francis has become sickly and frail. Nevertheless he clambers slowly through beech and pine forests high among crags of Mount La Verna in northern Italy. There, in a lengthy hermitage, he prays from before dawn till after sunset. He sleeps in a cavern. He blesses birds that he hears darting in treetops: "Bless you, my sister, little goldfinch." Then he leaves the few loyal friars who still accompany him, and he gropes his way alone to the other side of the chasm for a forty-day vigil. His body throbs with pain. Bleeding sores and lesions afflict him. Centuries later some scholars will propose that he has suffered from leprosy, resulting from many years of holding, bathing, and feeding victims of that disease. Near-blindness also plagues him, most likely from trachoma contracted in Egypt. During his solitary vigil Francis—a hurt, grizzled man of forty-three beseeching God in the darkness—clasps his hands and mutters impassioned prayers.

He prays through long days and nights. "Dear God of Heaven, though I am not worthy I sing your praise." Dizzy with hunger and fatigue, knees aching from hours of kneeling on stone, fiercely driven, he casts open his heart and his soul in surrender. "Christ my Lord, forgive me, I beg only to serve you." Then, after many days, a sudden blast of luminance: an angel with the face of Christ, its hands and feet spiked to a wooden cross, its six wings fanning the air.

What must it be like to pray ardently to Christ and have him appear? Perhaps Francis weeps. Perhaps he faints. Perhaps he gasps in awe.

After this vision Francis stumbles back to the pine grotto. He blinks with ruined eyes, his dirt-crusted hands and naked feet chapped and oozing, his unlaundered burlap tunic dank with sweat. Returned to his friars he grins exultantly. They catch their breath. It seems to them that Francis, enfeebled by malnutrition and disease, with blood seeping from the side of his bony chest and raw wounds in his hands and feet, now bears the Stigmata of Christ's wounds from the cross.[50]

*   *   *

Francis is not the only person experiencing mystical encounters, of course. In an age of materialism, corruption, and strife, many spiritually sensitive people in thirteenth-century Europe turn inward, seeking God. Mystical experience permeates the atmosphere. Arguably, it will help lead the way for the Protestant Reformation three centuries later, as devout Catholics in the 1200s discover that they can directly engage a sacred reality without intermediaries of priest or pope. Glancing at the Europe of this era we get a sense of the diversity and fervor that mark the mystical activities there:

Dwelling in Francis's native Umbria are not only his disciple Giles, an ecstatic contemplative, but the extraordinary mystic Angela di Foligno, a widow who lives in ascetic devotion to the crucified Christ and whose book, *Memorial*, recounts her intense visions, suffering, and revelation of thirty steps in the soul's ascent to God. There is Thomas Gallus in Italy as well and, in the German fiefdoms, friar David of Augsburg. Another German friar, who will later become one of the greatest Christian mystics, is born around 1260 and by century's end is studying in Paris: Meister Eckhart.

Celibate laywomen called Beguines live in their own spiritual communities within Dutch provinces of the northern Holy Roman Empire. Known as "women troubadours of God," many write rapturous poems about the soul's yearning for the Divine, similar in their passion and lyricism to Rūmī's. Other mystical poets such as Beatrijs of Nazareth, a Cistercian nun, and other women mystics such as Hadewijch and Mechthild of Magdeburg live in Antwerp. And there are many more women and men throughout Europe finding profound insight and fulfillment through direct encounters with the sacred via mystical paths to God, similar to Francis. Hundreds join far-flung groups of beatific seekers such as the Waldensians and the Humiliati, operating outside of established churches.[51]

In Europe's westernmost region of Spain, Christian knights following the battle of Las Navas de Tolosa in 1212 have seized the kingdoms of Navarre, Castile, and Aragon from the Muslims, and in those Spanish realms unorthodox spiritual activities now flourish among both Christians and Jews. (Sufis flourish as well, despite the Christian conquest; this is the era of the greatest of all Sufi masters, *shaykh* Ibn al-'Arabī.) Ramon Llull, the notable Christian visionary, traveler, and prolific author who admires Francis of Assisi, and whose "combinatory Art" utilizes elements of both Jewish mysticism and a metaphysics formulated by Ibn al-'Arabī, is born in Majorca in 1232 and later dies there, after wandering Europe, at the age of eighty-four. The ecstatic kabbalist Abraham Abulafia, born in Spain in 1240, also travels widely, and his mystical Judaism merges with Sufism among followers in Palestine. In Barcelona, an authority on the esoterica of Kabbalah named Nahmanides writes *Commentary on the Pentateuch* and plays a central role in establishing Kabbalistic mysticism as a Jewish theology in Spain. In Spain, too, thirteenth-century Kabbalah finds a unique voice in Moses de León, whose *Zohar*, a sprightly blend of Torah commentary, erotic poetry, numerology, parody, and experimental narrative, written in Aramaic and considered a mother lode of Kabbalistic lore, appears in the Castile region around 1280.[52]

Yet for spiritual seekers in the West many centuries later, Francis will tower above them all, with his equally lofty contemporaries Rūmī and Dōgen.

*　　*　　*

The year following Francis's vision of the crucified, six-winged angel, in 1225, Dōgen also undergoes a transformative spiritual experience. After living as a monk at an outlying monastery on Mt. T'ien-T'ung, for the past two years he has trekked alone past rice fields and hamlets in the Zhe River valley of southern China, searching from temple to temple, seeking a teacher who could help him find his own true path to the Dharma. Like monks of the T'ang Dynasty in the "Golden Age" of Ch'an Buddhism four hundred years earlier, he has carried only a patchwork bag and his bowl as he has tramped to the next village and knocked at its temple gate. Staying for a day or a few weeks he has taken meals, meditated, met with lackluster teachers, and left. Like the T'ang monks, too, he has roamed dirt paths of rural byways. He has paused to chat with elderly women at their roadside tea huts or with peasant farmers. Unlike those earlier monks, however, he has moved through mountains increasingly denuded of their forests, the trees fed into blast furnaces to fire China's booming iron industry. Roaming the barren slopes of this landscape, Dōgen has felt a growing discouragement. Hoping to find a vibrant Buddhism in the village temples, he has found instead the same malaise he experienced in Japan, with its wealthy, complacent priests and slothful students. Chagrined, he has nearly given up. He has thought, "Now what do I do?" He even has considered booking passage on a merchant sailboat back to Japan.

Finally he hears rumors about a Ch'an elder of grit and integrity, a Cao-Dong (or Southern School) monk named Ju-Ching—sometimes spelled "Rujing"—who serves as the new abbot back at Mt. T'ien-t'ung. When spring arrives, Dōgen travels again and finds him. The tough old abbot in his threadbare robes impresses Dōgen instantly. Unlike most Buddhists in China or Japan, corrupted by worldly desires, this man—clear-eyed, dynamic, and fearless—spurns pomp and luxuries, rejects rivalries between sects, and scorns the favors of royalty. A sort of Buddhist version of Francis, he lives a life of penury in the mountains. He also sits in meditation, practicing with unremitting dedication, often starting in a moonlit hall in the hours before daybreak and continuing until eleven at night. "Just sit," he demands, "and liberate mind and body." At last Dōgen has discovered his true teacher.

The young student sits with almost savage intensity. Within three years a moment of enlightenment—as powerfully transforming as Francis's experiences of the speaking Christ at San Damiano or of the crucified angel at La Verna—causes the "self" of the young Dōgen to drop away and, in that same instant, awakens him into radiant realization of Buddha-nature. It happens like this: a monk seated next to Dōgen has dozed off during the early morning meditation. Ju-Ching roars at the monk: "In meditating you must cast off body and mind! How can you sleep?" Hearing this, Dōgen's entire being bursts open in brilliant clarity and a calm joy. No "Dōgen" exists; instead, simple, luminous awareness, wholly alive, fully present and alert. For many months he has been spiritually preparing for such a moment and, in Ch'an terms, has become "ripe" for this instant of awakening. Later that morning, in Ju-Ching's private quarters, Dōgen offers incense. Probing, Ju-Ching queries him: "Why do you light the incense stick?" Dōgen feels aglow. He has sprung himself free. "My body and mind," he replies, "are cast-off."

That autumn of 1225, Dōgen becomes the first monk from Japan officially recognized in China as a dharma heir in the ranks of Ch'an Buddhist teachers.[53]

Near the end of that same year, Francis, ailing, sightless, close to death, invents the words and melody of "The Canticle of Brother Sun." He rasps them aloud. A paean of gratitude for the beauty and generosity of wind and water and stars in this world of constant perishing and renewal, he sings it as a song of delight composed in mortal agony. "Be praised, my Lord, with all Your creatures….Be praised, my Lord, for Sister Moon and the stars! / In the sky You formed them bright and lovely and fair…."[54]

For weeks he lies grimacing in pain. He withstands the tortures of medieval European medicine as physicians poke heated iron rods, glowing red, at his temples, or slice his veins, or pour stinging rock salt and egg yolks into his blind eyes in efforts to heal him. While doctors heat the rods for yet another excruciating round of therapy, Francis asks for consideration from his "Brother Fire." Speaking to the flames he says, "My brother, noble and useful among all creatures as you are, be courteous to me in this hour for I have always loved you and still do. I beg our Creator, who made you, to temper your heat so that I can bear it."[55] As the last of his health crumbles, Francis whispers the final verse of the "Canticle," in which he welcomes Sister Death. He prays ceaselessly. He dictates his "Testament."

"Since I cannot speak much because of my weakness and pain, I wish briefly to make my purpose clear to all my brothers," he murmurs. "I wish them always to love one another as I have loved them; let them always love and honor our Lady Poverty; and let them remain faithful and obedient to the bishops and clergy of holy mother Church."[56]

Soon after, he asks his brethren to lay him naked on the ground. He stretches his emaciated, sore-ridden, broken body in the form of a cross.[57]

Starting with nothing but faith in his life's mysterious calling, he had chosen to follow the Church as far as his conscience could bear, and beyond that to follow only God. He had chosen to live not like many of the Christians around him, but like Jesus. Owning nothing he had walked freely, in grace. In his brief life he had held lepers in his arms and bid peace to villagers and blessed all creatures. He had taught chastely a young woman, Clare, who charmed him and lived as his spiritual twin among her community of women while Francis preached and sang in the towns and countryside. He had traveled abroad and in warring camps he had befriended a traditional enemy, a great Muslim sultan. He had suffered hardships and yet he inspired an order of Franciscans who espoused his principles of poverty and goodwill. If, in the end, he seemed the only one who had not betrayed those principles, that too followed the tradition of Jesus forsaken by weaker disciples—the same Jesus experienced directly by Francis in his charged mystical encounters.

Now, in 1226, at the age of forty-five, the little "Fool for God" is dead. Francis had challenged the Church through the fierce example of a humble life. Two years after his death, that same Church canonizes him as a saint.

Dōgen returns to Japan in 1227, fervent with a new mission. "I came back to Japan with the hope of spreading the teaching and saving sentient beings—a heavy burden on my shoulders," he admits later.[58] Yet he feels eager to begin.

His teacher Ju-Ching had counseled him to publicize the Chinese form of Buddhism that in Japan would become known as Sōtō Zen; to shun cities and seek refuge in the mountains; to avoid the palaces of kings and ministers. Dōgen, always headstrong and independent, resists at first those last two pieces of advice. When his ship returns to Japan he travels directly to the imperial capital of Kyoto. A harsh lesson awaits him.

Arriving at the Rinzai Zen temple there he finds, as Francis had found so often in Italy, lazy monks indulging in fine clothes and treasures. Dōgen immediately writes *Fukan-zazengi* ("General Advice on the Principles of Zazen"), a ringing and revolutionary endorsement of the "just sit and liberate body and mind" techniques he had learned in China from Ju-Ching. Students excited by his vigor and freshness and his reformist zeal soon flock to Dōgen. His fame grows. So, too, does resentment from orthodox Rinzai Zen, Shingon, and Tendai Buddhists. Such resentment is no small matter. Many Japanese Buddhist monasteries house warrior-monks ready to battle any perceived foe.

Dōgen is now thirty years old. Realizing that his teacher's advice had been wise, he abandons Kyoto, a capital not only riven by doctrinal feuds, but rocked by earthquakes and famine. Dōgen and his new disciples move to the countryside, to bamboo thickets and copses of mixed pine and maples on a hillside of the Uji River plain near Fukakusa. There, in 1230, they move into a temple. Under Dōgen's supervision they slowly transform it. His workers repair tile roofs and eaves. In 1233 they open it as a Zen practice center called Kannondori. But Dōgen wants to create a monastery like Ju-Ching's in China. A few years later he reconfigures floor plans. Workers build new walls of plastered stone and paper screens. Finally the monks place black cushions for *zazen* meditation. In 1236 Dōgen realizes his goal: he opens the wooden gates of the first authentically Chinese-style Zen monastery in his native country, the first designed specifically for *zazen*. He calls it Kōshōhōrin-ji temple. It proves to be an epochal event.[59] In his opening lecture he explains that while practicing in China he had "dropped body and mind" in his enlightenment experience, and that he has returned to Japan "empty-handed," with no robes or relics or scrolls, only a clear mind. He then recites two verses he has composed, the last ending with the line, "The rooster crows at dawn." It is indeed a new day.[60]

At Kōshō-ji, Dōgen ink-brushes onto scrolls the first chapter of his masterwork the *Shōbōgenzō,* or *Treasury of the True Dharma Eye.* In it, he answers the question that has driven his spiritual quest since adolescence: each person indeed possesses from birth the original Buddha-nature, or enlightenment, he writes, "but it is not actualized without practice, and it is not experienced without realization."[61] How best to experience this realization? Through intense and unremitting meditation practice of *zazen*. Dōgen awes his monks by tireless personal example. He probably seems both visionary reformer and the medieval version of a drill sergeant. He teaches them that daily life and enlightenment are the same.

Seated on rice-straw *tatami* mats at Kōshō-ji he also records on scrolls his insights regarding aesthetics, epistemology, metaphysics. Many of these scrolls become fascicles of the *Shōbōgenzō,* one of the most magnificent works of Japanese philosophical literature. Among the more than sixty chapters composed during this period are his mind-bending "Uji," or "Being-Time," and his incomparable "Sansui kyō," or "Mountains and Rivers Sutra," with lines such as, "When you investigate mountains thoroughly, this is the work of mountains. Such mountains and waters of themselves become wise persons and sages." At Kōshō-ji he writes as well his earthy, practical, yet subtle "Tenzo Kyōkun," or "Instructions to the Cook," and drafts commentaries to scores of *kōans,* artfully designed to blast away the reader's illusions of selfhood, separation, and duality. Throughout the *Shōbōgenzō* Dōgen keeps his mind cogent, meticulous, and exact, while allowing it a full range of audacity and play. He flips standard Buddhist definitions of words upside-down. He tests language. He holds antitheses of Relative and Absolute in dynamic equipoise, shifting attention to one, then the other, returning always to a state of hyper-charged suspension.

Dōgen also writes poems at Kōshō-ji: "Every morning the sun rises in the east; / Every night, the moon sets in the west; / Clouds gathering over the foggy peaks; / Rain passes through the surrounding hills and plains."[62] And he paints a self-portrait: young man in his black robe, hair cropped to stubble, strong jaw and cheekbones, eyes gazing at the harvest moon.[63]

By this time Rūmī lives in the gracious Anatolian city of Konya, the Seljuk capital in present-day Turkey, a hundred miles inland from the Mediterranean in the high central plateau region of dry grasslands, oak and evergreen forests, lakes, and volcanic mountains. A luxuriantly bearded, vigorous man with bright eyes, Rūmī wears the turban and robes of a scholar and public official. He loves to saunter among his neighborhood's minarets and arbors, the street stalls, the baths, the taupe facades with arched doors. In winter he trudges Konya's streets in heavy snowfall, gazing at drifts along the city's fortress walls and whitened turrets of Sultan Alā ad-Dīn's palace atop the citadel. In summer heat he roves bazaars where camel caravans unload figs and raisins and olive oil and racks of dried fish carried from towns along the Black Sea. Five times throughout the day Rūmī ducks into the Alâeddin—the Great Mosque, capacious enough to accommodate four thousand prayerful men among its pillars—or one of the city's other mosques. There on his prayer rug he kneels toward Mecca and prays. He recites the *shahada*: "There is no god but Allah, and Muhammad is His messenger." Back on the avenues he greets merchants wearing fezzes, or Christian priests in their cassocks, or young schoolboys, or the goat drivers, or the bearded rabbis from the synagogues, or the wine vendors he knows by name, or robed government clerks scuttling toward gates of the palace grounds. Rūmī is listed as a doctor of the Law belonging to the Hanafi school, his family and his legal career flourishing. Townspeople come to his home office to settle disputes: who is the rightful owner of this flock of sheep? Is this marriage contract binding? According to *Shari'ah,* which brother inherits this apricot orchard?

Also in that year of 1231 Rūmī's father dies. The elder Walad had enjoyed the patronage of the Seljuk king, who had grandly bestowed on him the title "Sultan of men of knowledge." Rūmī now assumes at the age of twenty-four his father's duties in the *madrasah*. Unlike Dogen, who lost his father at the age of two, and unlike Francis, who rebelled against his merchant father and renounced the family business, Rūmī has been decisively influenced by his paternal heritage. Not only does Rūmī consider his father a mentor and a great teacher of *Tasawwuf,* of Sufism; he also emulates the literary style of his father's book the *Ma'arif,* which he studies assiduously following the elder's death.[64]

The next year, 1232, Rūmī starts his own Sufi training in earnest. Having mastered the principles of exoteric Islam as showcased in the legalistic doctrines of the *Shari'ah*, Rūmī now begins the long path— the *tariqa*—of mastering the esoteric, inward truth of Islam, the *haqiqa*, as first revealed by the Prophet. As an initiate training with the Sufi *shaykh* Burhān al-Dīn Muḥaqqiq Tirmidhī, who had been one of his father's chief disciples, Rūmī refines his already advanced knowledge of Islamic mysticism and its doctrines of the soul's surrender to Allah. He devotes himself to the "stations of the Way," including repentance, renouncement, trusting self-abandonment to God, endurance, contentment; he devotes himself as well to "states of the Way": desire for God, love, contemplation, proximity to God, intimacy.[65] He studies with Tirmidhī until the master's death in 1240. In his pursuit of mystical knowledge Rūmī also leaves his wife and children frequently to trek southward into Syria, following the watercourse of the Euphrates then striking across deserts where heated winds blow sand over the wadis of the high plateau. He crosses mountains of naked rock. He descends into walled cities of mosques and date palms. There he studies esoteric Islam at elite seminaries. He learns the mystical theology of his Spanish contemporary Ibn 'Arabi and others. He offers prayers to God and salutations to the Prophet, "friend of God" and symbol of the Light of the Prime Intellect. When he returns to Konya as a Sufi adept within the *silsila*, the chain of initiation linking masters and disciples, Rūmī gains regional fame as a preacher of the Qur'an and scholar of Islamic jurisprudence.

For the next four years he pursues his mystical practices and preaches at local mosques while living the decorous, respectable life of a lawyer. We may imagine him seated on plush carpets beneath intricate tiled mosaics and vases of red poppies, reading bound codices and unfurled scrolls dense with legal tenets of the *Shari'ah*, contemplating the revelation of Divine Will in earthly laws. Or puffing serenely on a water-pipe while listening to his sons recite their lessons. Or petting his cat in the garden. Or scenting his beard with rosewater before dining on minted lamb.

Following his wife's death, he marries again. He fathers two more children. Rūmī seems immersed in family life and a prosperous career, even amid political turmoil engulfing Anatolia.[66]

Soon, however, his life will smash open.

While Rūmī quietly studies Sufi mysticism and practices Islamic law in Konya, Dōgen—at the other end of Asia, seven thousand miles to the east, near the broad rice flats of Fukakusa, Japan—also is nearing a transformative crisis.

At his innovative Kōshōhōrin-ji monastery, Dōgen has been welcoming men and women of all social classes, from tattered peasants to shopkeepers to nobles in *yukata* or in jasmine-scented kimonos. He greets any person who wishes to enter the candlelit hall and staunchly pursue the Dharma Way by means of his uncompromising, direct technique of sitting in meditation. Kōshō-ji soon becomes a powerful Buddhist center. By opening its gates Dōgen has established something new; although he eschews the constrictions of labels, including that of "Zen school" or even "Buddha mind school," before long he becomes known as the founder of Zen's Sōtō sect in Japan.[67]

One of his lectures at Kōshō-ji consists, in its entirety, of a brief poem celebrating the loveliness of the temple and its surrounding landscape and the freedom of its sangha community: "The gentle hues of spring are / Everywhere apparent in this eastern paradise; / In heaven or on earth, / The season's beauty is nowhere / More fully realized / Than right here."[68]

Many days, when not meditating in *zazen* or giving lectures to monks and nuns or tending to affairs of the temple—when not receiving reports from the cook about rice stockpiles in the kitchen, or from the head monk about the need to buttress a zendo's roof beam before winter snowfall—Dōgen sits crosslegged with his brush and sumi ink and works on the *Shobogenzo*'s pages, dabbing paper scrolls with flawless calligraphy.

Yet problems mount. As more students arrive and as Kōshō-ji Sōtō Zen Temple grows in influence, rankling jealousy and unyielding antagonism from orthodox Tendai and Shingon Buddhist sects also increase. The Rinzai Zen temples, too, resent Dōgen's Sōtō Zen approach and his popularity. By 1243, Dōgen begins to remember his old teacher's advice: find sanctuary in the mountains.[69]

The year 1244 proves momentous for both Dōgen and Rūmī. The Japanese Zen teacher decides to leave behind all that he had built so painstakingly at Kōshō-ji. Dōgen leads his monks and nuns on a trek far into the distant mountain wilderness of Echizen, a hushed, isolated region of high peaks and deep snows on the western seacoast of Japan. Here, close to the whitecapped summit of sacred Mt. Hakusan, in rugged land roamed by deer and bears, near the ocean and its rocky sea cliffs and its storms but far from the petty bickering and corruption of Kyoto, Dōgen in his mid-forties starts all over again. Financed by a wealthy patron he builds a new Chinese-style temple monastery. Lay disciples chop trees. They plane logs and haul stones. They cart loads of roof tiles and supplies. When they finish the main building, Dōgen names it Eihei-ji, the "Temple of Eternal Peace." The name suggests Dōgen's longing to find freedom, at last, from religious strife and urban chaos.

In its remote alpine forests, Eihei-ji monastery serves as a small, exemplary community for hearty pioneers and spiritual seekers. Dōgen establishes it for men and women, peasants and merchants, samurai and nobles from throughout medieval Japan who wish to renounce conventional society and live harmoniously together as monks and nuns, undertake a stalwart practice of *zazen* and, without compromise, seek individual awakening. (More than 750 years later Dōgen's Eihei-ji temple remains today a headquarters of Sōtō Zen not only for the Japanese, but for practitioners throughout the world.)[70]

Poems written at Eihei-ji reflect the "eternal peace" that Dōgen seeks. "Crimson leaves / Whitened by the season's first snow— / Is there anyone / Who would not be moved / To celebrate this in song?"[71]

Meanwhile in that same year of 1244 the staid legal scholar Rūmī, a responsible, middle-aged family man of thirty-seven, experiences an event both shattering and euphoric. It changes him irrevocably. This spiritual breakthrough proves as awesome as Dōgen's "casting-off of body and mind" or Francis's visions of Christ. Rūmī meets an old wandering black-robed dervish who arrives that autumn in Konya, a teacher named Shams al-Din from the city of Tabrīz in the land known today as Iran.

Rūmī undergoes a stunning mid-life change. For years he has met his official obligations while pursuing academic study of Sufi mysticism. Something deep within him must have been feeling ravenous, though, for real experience, for liberation. Meeting Shams is the explosive catalyst.

Rūmī recognizes in Shams not only a kindred spirit, but a dazzling mentor, an emancipator. No more books: here, before him, stands the embodiment of sacred Love, brilliantly alive. This encounter bursts Rūmī's arcane Sufi mysticism into the open through a vast outpouring of ecstatic poems. "I was the country's sober ascetic, I used to teach from the pulpit," he later will recollect. "But destiny made me one of Thy hand clapping lovers." In hundreds of *ghazals*—a traditional verse form written in Persian—a blissful Rūmī hails the gray-bearded vagabond Shams as a divine Sufi saint, the image of the Sun, of the Beloved, of Allah. In a verse of his *Dīwān-e Shams-e Tabrīzī*, Rūmī gushes, "Passion for that Beloved took me away from erudition and reciting the Qur'an until I became as insane and obsessed as I am."[72]

Rūmī devotes himself to his new teacher as scrupulously as Dōgen had devoted himself to his teacher Ju-Ching in China twenty years earlier, but with far greater passion and fervid emotional attachment. The pair of Sufi mystics becomes inseparable. As the air chills and oak leaves brown and turn brittle through November, Rūmī and Shams talk endlessly, shunning meals, or sit in wordless rapture. Rūmī ignores fellow scholars and political colleagues, friends and family, students and legal clients.[73] "The raucous parrots / laugh," he writes, "and we laugh inside laughter, // the two of us on a bench in Konya, yet / amazingly in Khorasan and Iraq as well, // friends abiding this form, yet also // in another outside of time, you and I."[74] They continue to sit in Shams' tiny room through the snowbound winter and into early spring, soulmates in devout communion.

While Rūmī rhapsodizes over Shams, the older man—considered a disreputable eccentric by the citizens of Konya—also adores Rūmī as the perfect spiritual companion he has long sought in his years of footloose roaming. Shams, like Dōgen's maverick Chinese teacher Ju-Ching, has no use for religious dogma or institutions. Though educated, he disdains intellectual understanding. Wild and ragged, Shams blazes with intensity. Rūmī begins to emulate him. But as the resentment of Rūmī's students and fellow townspeople toward the strange visitor grows more wrathful, and as they begin to make threats, the unpredictable Shams suddenly vanishes. Rūmī feels devastated.[75]

His anguish is as searing, no doubt, as the grief young Dōgen endured when his mother died, and which inspired the boy's spiritual preoccupation with the nature of impermanence and death. Rūmī pours out hundreds of verses, aching with yearning and with the bewildered shock of losing the Beloved. "Separation and parting from Thee is difficult, oh Beloved, especially after Thy embrace!" "The scroll of my heart extends to Eternity-without-end, inscribed from first to last, 'Do not leave me!'" "A thousand fires and smokes and heartaches—and its name is Love! A thousand pains and regrets and afflictions—and its name is Beloved!" Heartsick lines such as these become the core of the huge collection of Rūmī 's verses in the *Dīwān-e Shams-e Tabrīzī*.[76]

During the next two years Rūmī, still bereft, continues to write poems effusively as he longs for his saintly friend and mentor, a longing which for Rūmī symbolizes the heart's thirst for God.

In Japan, meanwhile, Dōgen in the final years of his life is writing many of his own verses, poems vastly different from Rūmī's in style but with similar devotion to seeking the "original home," the

Absolute: "Because the flowers blooming / In our original home / Are everlasting, / Though springtimes may come and go / Their colors do not fade." When not instructing his monks, Dōgen sits morning *zazen* on a rock ledge under the cedars or walks shaded mountain glens along a tumbled brook. In his room he composes several chapters of the *Shōbōgenzō* and numerous monastic treatises of the *Eihei Kōroku* during these years at his mountain temple, moving tranquilly through the seasons: "In the spring, cherry blossoms, / In the summer the cuckoo, / In autumn the moon, and in / Winter the snow, the clear cold."[77]

In 1247 Shams returns to the streets of Konya. Rūmī had learned that Shams had gone to the Syrian capital of Damascus, and Rūmī, overjoyed, had dispatched his eldest son to persuade the dervish and Sufi master to come back. When Shams returns the two friends once more become inseparable. But old resentments flare among Rūmī's followers. Rūmī arranges for Shams to marry one of the girls in his household, and Shams loves her deeply, but when the girl dies in 1248 Shams vanishes again, this time forever. One of Rūmī's younger sons may have murdered him secretly, hating Shams as a pest and interloper.

Again Rūmī becomes disconsolate. Unaware that his friend may have been slain, Rūmī hikes into Syria, searching for Shams. We may imagine him querying shepherds in tents near reed marshes along the Euphrates, or pausing in oasis villages far to the south, in the sand and scrub of desert foothills, asking camel drivers if they have seen the glowering holy man in the black robes. We may imagine him roaming narrow alleys of Damascus, desperately scanning faces of passersby for the visage of his Divine Friend, looking in the silk markets, the bake shops, in shanties of bladesmiths at their forges, glancing at men gathered among vendors of huumus or roast mutton in the hour before *muzzeins* call the faithful, roaming past the Barada River, shouting "Shams! Shams!" in the plaza of the Great Mosque of the Umayyads.

We know that Rūmī pours forth passionate verses of lamentation and craving for the Beloved.

When Rūmī returns to Konya from a second trip into Syria, however, he seems at peace. He has found Shams. Rūmī has found him not in the exterior world, but within himself, eternally bright and alive. Lover and Beloved, he now realizes, unite perpetually as one.[78]

In 1248, the year of Shams' final disappearance, Dōgen in western Japan sometimes ventures out of his forest refuge to the castle of Kamakura's regional shogun when invited to give Buddhist teachings, but otherwise rarely leaves the mountains of Eihei-ji Temple. He sips tea. He shuffles on paths among wet cedars, as drizzle and fogs roil the high peaks. He gives counsel to students. Daily he sits before his assembled monks and nuns in the great hall, silently intent on meditation.

He marks his fiftieth birthday, an advanced age for the medieval era, in the year 1250. The emperor awards Dōgen a sumptuous purple robe of finest sateen; Dōgen courteously accepts the gift but refuses to wear it. "If an old monk here wore a purple *kesa*, he would be laughed at by monkeys and cranes." He prefers the dark patchwork robes of a monk.[79]

In 1253, infirm and sickly, Dōgen journeys back to Kyoto to seek medical treatment. "Like a blade of grass, / My frail body / Treading the path to Kyoto, / Seeming to wander / Amid the cloudy mist on Kinobe Pass." His illness proves too advanced. He knows he is approaching the "Yellow Springs," the traditional Chinese expression for death, a phrase used also in Japanese literature.[80]

On a late summer day in Kyoto, the city of his aristocratic birth, Dōgen sits *zazen* a final time, surrounded by his closest students. While seated in the meditation posture he spontaneously composes his death poem, in the tradition of Zen teachers facing their last moments: "Fifty-four years lighting up the sky./ A quivering leap smashes a billion worlds./ Hah!/ Entire body looks for nothing./ Living, I plunge into Yellow Springs."[81]

Rūmī will live for another twenty years. Once a stiffly proper, bookish lawyer, Rūmī now spends many of his hours devising and singing verses, or immersed in *sama*—the mystical Sufi rites of music and whirling dance. Eyes closed, arms extended, his right palm open to heaven, Rūmī plants one foot firmly on the earth and twirls in blissful meditation.

About 1250, after experiencing divine union with Allah through means of his heart's eternal bond with Shams, the saintly Beloved and Image of God, Rūmī finds another spiritual friend. Walking through the goldsmith's bazaar in Konya, Rūmī hears the bright ringing of a mallet in the shop of an acquaintance, the Sufi adept Ṣalāḥ al-Dīn Zarkūb. Allured by the rhythm, he spreads his arms and with eyes clenched shut begins to spin slowly in spiritual rapture. Ṣalāḥ al-Dīn joins him. Both men turn round and round in the silent, unhastening dance of Sufi dervishes.

Again townspeople are scandalized. Rūmī and the illiterate but spiritually awakened Ṣalāḥ al-Dīn spend years together in joyous spiritual communion, and Rūmī marries his oldest son to Ṣalāḥ al-Dīn's daughter. During this period Rūmī lives ascetically with his second wife Kera Khatun and their children. As he has done so often before, he fasts and prays to Allah. He reads the Qur'an to discern its encoded, mystical secrets. He intones praises of the Prophet. He goes on spiritual retreat, *khalwa*, and practices *dhikr*, the recollection of Divine Names through litany and invocation. He renders decisions as an Islamic legal expert. He helps impoverished people of Konya find work (rather than giving all of his possessions to them, as Francis had). He receives wealthy, powerful visitors, speaks with modest blacksmiths, wool carders, and bakers, and teaches men and women who become Sufi disciples. He tends his garden of roses and poppies. He visits the baths. He hosts night-long religious celebrations, with mesmerizing, sinuous music of tambours, hand-drums, reed flutes and zithers, and enraptured, spinning dances. Rūmī establishes the Mevlevi order of whirling dervishes. He also continues to rove the streets of Konya creating and exclaiming verses. In 1256 a companion, a *sheykh* named Hosamoddin Chalabi, begins to record these; the verses eventually become the sprawling compendium of Rūmī's work known as the *Mathnawī*. When Rūmī's spiritual companion Ṣalāḥ al-Dīn dies in 1258, the master adopts Hosamoddin as his new mystical Friend.

Although civil wars and Mongol incursions continue to wrack mid-thirteenth century Anatolia, Rūmī manages to live serenely through his last decade. He picnics on languorous summer days with comrades and disciples and visits regional hot springs.

By 1273, at the age of sixty-six, Rūmī begins to weaken. That winter his health worsens. Friends, family, and disciples gather at his bedside. Rūmī comforts them with poems about death as a door to new life. One evening, at sunset, twenty years after Dōgen has passed to the "Yellow Springs," Rūmī dies.[82]

Grieving Muslims, Christians, and Jews from throughout the province hold a massive funeral.

They praise Rūmī as *Mawlānā*, or "master." Today, each year his admirers continue the tradition of celebrating December 17, the day Rūmī died, as his "wedding day," the date of his union with God.[83]

* * *

This is who Francis, Dōgen, and Rūmī were. Accomplished spiritual teachers, they endured hardships and triumphed in an age of dramatic changes and conflict. They also were mavericks. Their lives and mystical practices defied the orthodoxies of their established traditions. Francis, as a radical Christian reformer, worked independently of priesthood and monasteries. Dōgen lived outside of the mainstream

Japanese Buddhist power structure. Rūmī, an ecstatic Sufi adept, operated beyond the bounds of conventional Islam.

Although they were rebels who in some respects transcended their thirteenth-century era, Francis, Dōgen, and Rūmī also valued their spiritual heritage and continued to function within the distinctive milieus of their medieval societies. Each lived as a person of his time. It is precisely because of their passionate engagement with their own era that this trio of thirteenth-century mystics continues to appeal so powerfully to a new generation of spiritual seekers today. Contemporaries to each other in the Middle Ages, they often feel like our contemporaries as well.

Spiritual issues that preoccupied Francis, Dōgen, and Rūmī emerge in varying degrees as shared themes in their lives and works. As we see in the following chapter, five of the most fascinating include love, nature, the body, the role of women, and the balance of retreat with active involvement in the world.

These themes speak to us across centuries and feel modern. It is one reason that Francis, Dōgen, and Rūmī seem familiar and congenial. They engage us directly in their spiritual interests—topics which still concern us today—in language we understand.

Chapter Two

Speaking to Us Across Centuries

Love

In mystical communion the heart opens to love. Deeply transformed by mystic experience, Francis, Dōgen, and Rūmī each manifested love in his own original and characteristic manner.

Francis was deeply influenced by ideals of chivalry and courtly love. Those chivalric ideals, expressed in the troubadour lyrics that Francis had often sung as a young man, required a knight to pledge himself with perfect fidelity, chastity, and honor to a noble lady. Francis transformed this secular ideal of courtly love by casting it in sacred terms. He told anyone who would listen that he had pledged himself, as God's knight, to a supreme maiden, Lady Poverty. When others inquired about his drastic acts of self-denial, Francis replied that by performing such acts he was paying courtesies to her. By "Poverty," Francis meant mystical poverty—not only the giving away of all worldly possessions, such as clothes and food and bed and hearth, but the complete giving of self.[1] When ownership of self is renounced, then love pours forth unimpeded.

In mystical poverty, owning nothing that might distance him from God, destitute even of self, Francis in his sacred transformation of courtly love paid devoted homage to his Lady, and as his love radiated forth he became joyously rich in spirit. Though a beggar, he amassed the truest form of wealth. As he did so, he gave it away lavishly, a spendthrift of love. In the sacred economy, he saw his heart's bounty increase a thousandfold even as he relinquished all its riches, bestowing the largesse of his love on the most desperately needy.

The binding devotion of Francis to his Lady Poverty—a devotion rendered as courtly romance in the allegorical *Sacrum Commercium*, published in 1227, soon after Francis's death, and again in Canto XI of the *Paradiso*, in which Dante depicts Francis in holy matrimony with Lady Poverty[2]—freed him completely, and in this freedom he could devote himself to others. In loving service, he strove to live as Jesus had. His acts of love proved revolutionary.

For example, he embraced lepers. Outcasts who inspired revulsion and fear, lepers lived in quarantined huts far outside the walls of European medieval towns. They could approach other people only if they rang a bell. Legally, they were considered the walking dead. Powered by love, Francis not only embraced lepers; Bonaventure tells us that he washed their feet, bound up their sores, wiped the pus, cleansed them, kissed their wounds.[3] How could Francis embrace people considered, by law, already dead to the world? By dying, first, himself. The mystical death of the self liberated him to love even the most reviled and untouchable of God's creatures.

Other Christians had tended these pariahs, of course. A decade before Francis, one of the Beguines named Mary of Oignies and her husband had cared for victims of leprosy in present-day Belgium.[4] But Francis did not "tend" or "care for"—which implies separation, one individual helping another individual, with empathy but perhaps also with condescension or even an ostentatious display of pious virtue. Francis did not know separation. Because he had experienced the death of the individual ego, he gave his full being and his full presence. In those moments when he hugged and held and bathed the lepers, he did so in union, in complete identification, so that in a spiritual sense the lepers bathed and held and hugged him too; and in that embrace of suffering they wholly embraced the suffering of Christ on the cross. This is what made Francis unique.

But in that suffering, too, was joy. Not a fleeting, superficial happiness, but authentic joy, severely tested in misery and pain yet, at the core of his being, perpetually abiding. His love for all expressed itself as sweet civility and kindliness, as sublime courtesy. The word "courtesy," it should be recalled, derives from the etiquette of the royal "court" and shares an etymological pedigree with the "courtly love" Francis esteemed so highly.[5]

Accordingly, Francis set himself against no one he encountered. He did not fight heretics. He did not fight the Muslims who had taken Jerusalem. He expressed strong disdain for the lackluster monks of the Benedictines, Cluniacs, and Cistercians and the bishops and cardinals and popes besotted with their lust for power and lucre, but he did not fight them. Nor did he fight the vulgar, war-crazed, money-mad aristocrats of the embattled Italian provinces—those mighty ones who profited so handsomely and looked so comely and enjoyed the world's acclaim, but who reeked of leprosy in their souls. It was an inspired position for a radical reformer to take. In his mystic and truly selfless love Francis might argue on behalf of all that he perceived as just and true, and he might set an oppositional example in the way he lived, but he condemned no one.[6]

Francis accepted life as it came to him, cheerfully, tenderly, and unafraid. He took the world whole; it was God's, and despite everything it was good. Such a message, coming as it did in an age that emphasized God's divine wrath and His terrifying punishment of sinners, amazed people. "He loved," writes Pope Francis, who in our own twenty-first century has adopted the name of the "little saint of Assisi," and he was "deeply loved for his joy, his generous self-giving, his open-heartedness."[7]

Though Francis demonstrated every day the power of his active love, this did not preclude flashes of anger. Francis was not a goody-goody little saint. Like Jesus, who coldly challenged the hypocrite Pharisees or furiously drove the money-grubbers from his Father's temple, Francis could use anger righteously. Handed money, he threw it in a pile of cow manure. His friars were supposed to own nothing at all. When he returned from traveling and saw that, in his absence, they had spurned Lady Poverty by accepting a cozy house to live in, he indignantly climbed to the roof and began ripping out the tiles, hurling them to the ground. When a friar repeatedly asked to own a prayer book of his own, Francis finally grabbed the book and tossed it aside, scolded the friar by saying, "Next thing you'll want a throne to sit on so you can tell your brothers, 'Fetch me my prayer book,'" then scooped ashes from the campfire and dumped them over his own head, shouting, "This is my prayer book!"[8] That final gesture with the ashes, incidentally—a teaching spontaneous and direct and pure, tough but ultimately loving in its intent to shock the friar into awareness—was worthy of a Zen teacher. (Unfortunately we do not know if the friar experienced enlightenment at that moment.)

In the end, nearing death, blind, and suffering agonies of pain, Francis's words to his friars spoke of love: "Always love each other; always love Our Lady, Holy Poverty; always be faithful to the prelates and clerics of Holy Mother the Church."[9]

The active, loving ministry of Saint Francis to the needy, the wretched, the maimed and rejected people of society is wholly alien to the thirteenth-century Zen Buddhism of Dōgen. Indeed, it may be suggested that the revolutionary ethic of loving service that Francis enacted so faithfully has only now, in the late twentieth and early twenty-first centuries, arrived in Buddhism. The recent movement of "Socially Engaged Buddhism" encourages Zen, Tibetan, Theravada, and other Buddhists to work with loving hearts in prisons, hospices, homeless shelters, and soup kitchens; to labor on behalf of clean air and clean water and to preserve threatened species and to protect the endangered planet; to halt racism and the oppression of women; to discourage war; it is a movement that incorporates Franciscan values. It is a truly auspicious merging of East and West.

In his own era, however, Dōgen did not espouse an ethic of active love in service to the despairing masses. It is simply impossible to imagine Dōgen embracing a Japanese leper in an alley of Kyoto, or cleansing pus from a leper's sores and kissing the wounds. Dōgen's concern was exclusively for the welfare of his monastics. As their teacher his responsibility was to help guide them to enlightenment—with a love tempered by stern admonitions and discipline. Some of Dōgen's Japanese Buddhist contemporaries noticed this and criticized it as *engaku*, or self-enlightenment that ignores the suffering of others. They "saw exclusive Zen practice as narrow-minded Buddhism, deficient in social benefits," according to William M. Bodiford's *Sōtō Zen in Medieval Japan*.[10]

Still, if the standard Mahayana vow to "save all sentient beings" qualifies as love, then Dōgen incontestably was loving, though in this rather abstract and doctrinal way. Referring more specifically to Zen practice, Dōgen taught that when selfish ego becomes effaced through the enlightenment that arises through sitting *zazen*, then compassion arises naturally, with no "I" to impede it, no "me" or "mine" to separate it from others.

He insisted, in "Guidelines for Studying the Way," that "compassion is the basis of the various teachings." And Dōgen instructed his monastics to use "kind speech." This means, he wrote in "Bodhisattva's Four Methods of Guidance," that "when you see sentient beings you arouse the mind of compassion and offer words of loving care." In the same essay he urged his monastics to practice giving. "Not only should you make an effort to give, but also be mindful of every opportunity to give."[11]

The word "love" does not occur frequently in Dōgen's writings, but when it does his warmth and sincerity feel palpable. An excerpt from his "Instructions to the Cook" is especially poignant, given that Dōgen was orphaned at the age of seven:

> 'Kind mind' is parental mind. Just as parents care for their children, you should bear in mind the three treasures. Even poor or suffering people raise their children with deep love. Their hearts cannot be understood by others. This can become known only when you become a father or mother. They do not care whether they themselves are poor or rich; their only concern is that their children will grow up. They pay no attention to whether they themselves are cold or hot, but cover their children to protect them from the cold or shield them from the hot sun. This is extreme kindness.[12]

Ultimately, Dōgen manifested his love for others by selflessly bringing from China to Japan a meditation practice that he considered a true means of liberation from suffering. He shared it openly and generously with any person—man or woman, noble or peasant—who wished to ordain as a monk or a nun and learn. If somebody showed diligence and sincerity and kept the monastic vows, Dōgen was there for that person. His temple doors were open. Dōgen lovingly dedicated the fullness of his life to helping his monastics win release from the miseries of ego-bound existence. Despite hardships he did so with attentiveness and care, and he watched and guided his disciples with the "kind mind," the "parental mind," of which he wrote so movingly. In his secluded mountain monastery deep in the wilderness of Echizen he endeavored to change the world, one enlightened student at a time. It was a far cry from the active love and the ethic of loving service demonstrated by Francis, but it was love nevertheless, and authentic.

Rūmī was another matter entirely. The immediate image that occurs for most people today who hear the name "Rūmī" is that of a Persian poet intoxicated with ecstatic love. "It can easily be shown that Love ('ishq) is the central theme of all Rūmī's works," declares William C. Chittick in *The Sufi Path of Love: The Spiritual Teachings of Rumi*. "In Rūmī's view, Love totally dominates and determines the Sufi's inward and 'psychological' states."[13] That Love, of course, is the sacred rapture of the True Self for its Beloved, Allah.

As a Sufi, Rūmī knows that Love flows naturally when the veil of *nafs*, or ego, ceases to restrict it, when the petty self is torn away, annihilated in the act of *fanā*, and the True Self then freely endures, in *baqā*, within the Divine Beloved. This, of course, resembles the way Francis knows love and the way Dōgen knows compassion: as arising unimpeded when the ever-present selfishness of "me, me, me" vanishes.

Rūmī, also like Francis, uses the language of mystical poverty to express this lack of ego, this deprivation that leads to spiritual riches of Love. "Poverty unlocks the door—what a blessed key!" he exclaims in the *Dīwān-e*. And again: "The physician, poverty, sought and found my heart's ear. It whispered, 'Spread the good news: You have been delivered from the suffering of existence.'" (Interestingly, "spread the good news" is the exhortation of the Christian Gospels; delivery "from the suffering of existence" is the Third Noble Truth of the Buddha.) Continuing his theme of mystical poverty and Love, Rūmī writes, "No one will understand these mysteries of Thy Gentleness but he who comes out from the spiritual work without existence, obliterated by poverty." And in the *Mathnawī*: "When annihilation adorns a man because of his poverty, he becomes shadowless, like Muhammad." And from the *Fihi ma fihi*: "But when you enter the world of poverty and practice it, God bestows upon you kingdoms and worlds that you never imagined."[14] Chittick explains that Rūmī "often employs the term 'poverty' in a context showing that it is synonymous with 'annihilation' and 'non-existence.' The dervish is he who is 'poor' because he has nothing of 'his own.' *He is totally empty of selfhood.* The true 'poor man' is in truth the richest of all men, since, not existing himself, he subsists through the [True] Self."[15]

Empty of selfhood, becoming *faqr* ("poor" in Arabic), becoming *darwish* ("poor" in Persian, from which the word "dervish" originates), a person may authentically know and experience Love in all its forms. The Sufi, the lover, knows that Love courses throughout the universe, a vitalizing energy from the original act of Creation, and that all the living and non-living things of the world reflect that Love, which flows from Allah. "The creatures are set in motion by Love, Love by Eternity-without-beginning; the wind dances because of the spheres, the trees because of the wind," Rūmī writes in the *Dīwān-e*. Allah, the Hidden Treasure, who in His essence is One and Unknowable, created the universe of forms because He wished to make Himself known. Allah becomes partially known to humans through his attributes, and one of those attributes is Love.[16]

The Beloved, Allah, seeks the lover, while the true lover, in turn, desires to see, unveiled, the hidden face of the Beloved. (Compare St. John of the Cross: "Oh Night, that did so then unite / The Loved with his Beloved, / Transforming Lover in Beloved," from *The Dark Night of the Soul*.)[17] In Sufi terminology, when a seeker has climbed the spiritual ladder ascending through the nine celestial spheres of heaven, with a cleansed heart and purified intellect, and in selfless poverty, it becomes possible to enter the gardens of spring and grow blissfully drunk on the wine of Love and the kisses of the Beloved.[18]

For Rūmī, this journey into the gardens to see the face of Allah occurred when he found his *shaykh*—his saintly teacher—a man who seemed to him the mirror of the Beloved on earth: Shams-i-Tabrīzī. "Oh my moon, my bright candle!" wrote Rūmī in the *Dīwān-e*. "From the time I first saw Thy Face, wherever I sit I am joyful, wherever I go I dwell in the midst of roses."[19] Rūmī's intense outpourings addressed to the saintly Shams have, as their ultimate object, the Divine Lover. All of Rūmī's desire is for Allah. Drunk with spiritual passion, Rūmī delightedly and tirelessly shouts his love. Again from the *Dīwān-e*:

In truth, love for the Illuminator of hearts keeps lovers
    awake all night without food and sleep.
    Oh friend, if you are a lover, be like a candle:
Melt all night long, burn joyfully till morning!
He who is like cold weather in autumn is no lover –
    in autumn's midst the lover's heart is burning summer.
Dear friend, if you have a love you want to proclaim, then
    shout like a lover!
Shout! Shout! [20]

It is tempting, incidentally, to imagine what Francis and Dōgen might have thought if they could have read Rūmī's poems of ecstatic spiritual love. Francis, who as a young man had spent many nights reeling drunkenly from wine and shouting as a lover, in his rowdy days as Assisi's "Master of the Revels," probably would have found Rūmī's imagery familiar—though of course for Francis in his maturity, "wine" also would have had an entirely different significance, as the sacramental blood of Christ. Still, he would have understood that the Sufi was employing secular references for sacred purposes, much as Francis did himself in adopting the conventions of troubadours and courtly love to speak of God. Francis also enjoyed laughing and singing throughout his life, and could have responded easily to the gaiety in Rūmī's work. Moreover, in 1219 James of Vitry reported having seen "Brother Francis, who was rapt to such great ecstasy of drunkenness and fervor of spirit";[21] thus Francis knew firsthand the state of spiritual bliss and metaphorical intoxication that Rūmī described. Dōgen, on the other hand, experienced spiritual rapture very differently and used a different vocabulary. Rather than indulge a state of spiritual giddiness akin to inebriation he would have returned to Zen's clear and peaceful equilibrium. And, too, because he was raised in celibate monasteries since the age of twelve, and had foresworn all intoxicants when he took Buddhist precepts, the somber Dōgen most likely would have paused at lines of Rūmī's such as "The wine-worshippers are all busy with revelry – / listen to the strumming of the lute, oh body-worshipper!"[22] Still, he might have recognized the source of such lines in authentic experience of the sacred. He may have accepted them.

Rūmī's love was not exclusively spiritual, however. It rooted firmly in the mundane. Like Francis, he maintained an ethic of loving service, although it took another form. Rūmī frequently gave money to the poor or found jobs for the needy, in keeping with the Third Pillar of Islam, which is charity.[23] Each year Muslims must tithe one-fortieth of the value of all their possessions to the poor. Rūmī did so faithfully. He also, unlike Francis and Dōgen, cared not only for a group of disciples but for a large family of wife and children and relatives. He had numerous cherished friends as well. Rūmī's love flourished in this world, as much as it soared heavenward to Allah.

But it is the mystical love that stirs readers today. As Evelyn Underhill writes in her classic study, *Mysticism: A Study in the Nature and Development of Man's Spiritual Consciousness*, "The mystic life is a life of love."[24] For Rūmī and Dōgen and Francis, love and compassion resulted from their quests for Allah, for realized Buddha-nature, or for God, respectively, and love also sustained and energized those quests.

Nature

As mystics Francis, Dōgen, and Rūmī each responded with sensitivity and creative originality to the life-force and power of trees and blossoms and ripening fruits, to rivers and ponds, to mountain peaks, and to the myriad creatures inhabiting them. Each evinced a potent sense of harmony with the natural world.

In this regard Francis proved exceptional. "I believe that Saint Francis is the example par excellence of care for the vulnerable and of an integral ecology lived out joyfully and authentically," Pope Francis has written in his landmark 2015 encyclical on the environment, *Laudato Si'*. "He is the patron saint of all who study and work in the area of ecology."[25]

Saint Francis achieved something profoundly new in Western culture. Granted, the High Medieval world of the thirteenth century abounded in references to what philosophers called *natura naturans*, to nature in its teeming fecundity, God's creation sustaining itself in fertile cycles of renewal. Cathedrals throughout Europe in the 1200s featured not only the sculpted figures of saints and angels and cherubim, but images of the Green Man—a benign nature spirit, masked with acanthus leaves, bearded and mustached with vines and tendrils, clothed in foliage, a pagan god of the natural world, appropriated by the Church to symbolize resurrection. The mythological goddess Natura, a powerful deity of fecundity and renewal, remained popular in medieval Europe as well. In troubadour songs of courtly love the chosen lady often was described in terms familiarly employed in paeans to Natura herself.[26] And, too, European people of all social classes, both urban and rural, lived on intimate daily terms with the natural world: with snow, sun, and rain, with seed and harvest, with storks and magpies, with falcons, with horses and street dogs, with rats and lice, with the beech forests they were rapidly cutting to clear the land for grain.

Yet despite this immersion in nature, Westerners of the High Middle Ages still considered themselves superior to it. Medieval Europeans believed that humans—as descendants of Adam, who was granted dominion by God over the birds and fishes and beasts of the field—were divinely ordained to rule the rest of Creation. Francis of Assisi did not agree.

His revolutionary innovation was to perceive that humans live within a glorious extended family. Francis realized that our kin, whom we should love and treat with deference, are Brother Sun, and Sisters Moon and Stars, Brothers Wind and Air, Brother Fire, the Earth our mother, and Brother Ant, Sister Swallow, Brother Wolf and Sister Flowers and everything teeming and alive in God's creation, each jubilantly praising the Lord in its own distinctive and irreplaceable way.[27]

Francis did not simply talk about this. As he did with everything, he lived it, and he did so without compromise.

"He removed from the road little worms, lest they be crushed under foot," writes Friar Thomas of Celano, "and he ordered that honey and the best wines be set out for the bees, lest they perish from want in the cold of winter. He called all animals by the name *brother*, though among all the kinds of animals he preferred the gentle."

And more: he forbade the monks to chop down the entire tree when they cut wood, "so that it might have hope of sprouting again." Francis told the gardener to leave room at the borders of the vegetable plots for "the greenness of the grass and the beauty of the flowers," so that they "might announce the beauty of the Father of all things."

And still more: Francis talked to fire. Thomas of Celano relates that when doctors tried to cauterize the skin of his temples with a red-hot metal rod, Francis prepared for this medical torture by speaking softly to "Brother Fire" and asking it to be courteous with him. To Francis all of nature was alive and sentient and kindred.

Francis preached to the birds and released rabbits from traps and rescued lambs being taken to slaughter and returned fish to the water. He befriended pheasants and crickets. It was said that birds rested in his cupped palms. It was said that a savage wolf terrorized the village of Gubbio, and Francis approached him, called him "Brother Wolf," and tamed him.[28]

Astonishingly, Francis even dared to contradict—in writing—the standard Biblical authority of Genesis, which stated categorically that animals exist to serve man.

In the final stanza of his poem "The Praises of the Virtues," where no reader could possibly miss it, Francis turned this completely around. He wrote, "Obedience subjects a man / to everyone on earth, / And not only to men, / but to all the beasts as well / and to the wild animals, / So that they can do what they like with him, / as far as God allows them."[29] Somehow he avoided a charge of blasphemy from the papal offices in Rome.

"Francis tried to depose man from his monarchy over creation and set up a democracy of all God's creatures," writes Lynn White Jr. approvingly in his essay "The Historical Roots of Our Ecological Crisis." With Francis, "the ant is no longer simply a homily for the lazy, flames a sign of the thrust of the soul toward union with God; now they are Brother Ant and Sister Fire, praising the Creator in their own way."[30]

It is crucially important to understand that Francis was not simply a "nature lover" or "animal lover": he was a mystic, who could embrace Brother Mulberry Tree and Sister Rain for the same reason he could embrace Brother and Sister Lepers—because he had died to self, had burned away the pestering, interfering ego and could approach every earthly thing and every living creature without separation, with an utterly open heart, welcoming them with gratitude and exultant love. "He was a mystic and pilgrim," writes Pope Francis, "who lived in simplicity and in wonderful harmony with God, with others, with nature and with himself."[31]

Dōgen, too, was a nature mystic, but of a very different and very particular type—distinctly Japanese, and distinctly Zen. Dōgen's relationship to nature had both a sensory, emotional component and a philosophical component. The sensory and emotional aspect refers to his fondness for the natural world as he experienced it in his travels or in the mountain fastness of the rugged peaks of Echizen—the snowflakes, the moon, fireflies, a spider web, red leaves of autumn, a magpie, blanket of clouds, a mandarin duck, all of which appear in his poems. "Though mountains belong to the territory of the nation, they are entrusted to people who love the mountains," Dōgen wrote in the "Mountains and Waters Sutra" section of the *Shōbōgenzō*. [32] Dōgen did love them. He forsook Kyoto to build his "Temple of Eternal Peace" in the high, distant summits near the Sea of Japan, a remote and wild terrain. In doing so he adapted the spiritual practice of dwelling in a mountain hermitage, or *yamazato*, a venerable Japanese tradition based on the view of nature as both reflecting, and serving as inspiration for, the spiritual seeker. He did not go as a recluse. He went to the mountains and rivers he cherished in order to create a monastic community—one that would demonstrate, in daily life, the non-separation of human and nature. [33]

Dōgen's emotional response to nature also was informed by his practice of compassion as the awakening of the Bodhisattva Vow to save all beings: "Commiserate with a turtle in trouble, and take care of a sparrow suffering from injury," he wrote. "When you see the distressed turtle or watch the sick sparrow, you do not expect any repayment for your favor, but are moved entirely by your desire to help others." [34] The similarity to Francis here is striking.

The philosophical aspect of Dōgen's relationship to nature is, like everything in Dōgen's thought, subtle, complex, and, though steeped in traditional Buddhist teachings, thoroughly idiosyncratic. Though a nature mystic, Dōgen was not one in the Romantic sense; [35] Dōgen did not worship nature (which, after all, would imply a separation between the worshipper and the thing venerated). Nor did he seek to become absorbed in nature or to "lose himself" in contemplating pretty scenery. Nor was he a pantheist, nor did he consider nature sacred and the city profane (which would mean dualism), nor did he indulge in the sentimentalizing of nature so popular among his Japanese cohorts, with their wistful reveries of moon-gazing among the fallen plum blossoms. He was a nature mystic, however, in that he saw the world of mountains and waters clearly and directly, in their essential "thusness"—a Zen term for ultimate reality manifesting in "things-as-they-are"—and he could see them in this way because his enlightenment moments of "casting-off body and mind" had shown him how to displace the ego.

Dōgen's view of nature was, in its own way, as revolutionary as Francis's. Most people make a dualistic distinction between sentient and insentient and think of pine trees and chrysanthemums and pebbles and brooks as belonging to the latter category. Moreover, they assume that the insentient cannot communicate. Dōgen disagrees with such people, and in the *Shōbōgenzō* calls their assumption "contrary to the Buddha-way." Dōgen "revolts against such a conception of nature," according to Hee-Jin Kim in *Eihei Dōgen: Mystical Realist*. "From the standpoint of the Way, insentient beings do elucidate Dharma, not in human languages but in their own expressions (*dōtoku*). Hence they are 'alive' in their own way; in Dōgen's phraseology, the insentient beings are 'sentient.'"[36]

Here we are very close to the sentience of Francis's Brother Fire. To Dōgen, all existence—including the rocks and persimmons, the maples and the waterfalls, everything that comprises the world—is sentient and one with Buddha-nature. In Dōgen's words: "All living beings have buddha nature. Grass, trees, land, and earth are heart. As they are heart, they are living beings. As they are living beings they have buddha nature. Sun, moon, stars are all heart. As they are heart, they are living beings. As they are living beings, they have buddha nature."[37]

Human beings are inseparable from nature; nature and humanity cooperate in achieving enlightenment together. In Dōgen's words: "When you endeavor in right practice, the voices and figures of streams and the sounds and shapes of mountains, together with you, bounteously deliver eighty-four thousand [chanted teachings of the Buddha]. Just as you are unsparing in surrendering fame and wealth and the body-mind [to reach enlightenment], so are the brooks and mountains."[38]

"Dōgen dealt with many subjects of nature in his works," Kim writes, "such as mountains, waters, flowers, the moon, and the four seasons." However, the "love" of nature, in Dōgen's thought, is not a deification of nature but a radicalization of nature, Kim asserts.[39] That is, when Dōgen speaks of a "mountain" in the *Shōbōgenzō*, he is not speaking of it as an object viewed in dualistic relationship by a subject; nor is he speaking of the mountain as a concept formulated in the human mind, as an idea or a metaphor or a signifier ("Do not judge mountains by human standards," Dōgen insists.[40]) He means the mountain seen clearly in its specificity, in its thusness, in its ultimate reality manifesting through the "radical" and "total exertion of a single thing" in its own unique moment of being-time, as Kim says. "This is why Dōgen quotes the following from Yun-men Wen-yen (864-949): 'A mountain is a mountain; water is water.' This statement represents the essence of Zen itself." However, at each unique moment when the mountain is a mountain, not only the specific mountain but the entire universe is realized, in its interconnectedness and its dynamic flow of impermanence and its ultimate Emptiness. This is "nature in its selflessness," Kim says. "Only then is nature undefiled and natural."[41] To see nature in its selflessness, of course, requires a selfless viewer—and in that moment nature and viewer are united. This complete union is called in the Japanese literary tradition *muga*. Bashō, for example, would later express it boldly and freshly in his haiku.[42] To experience mountains and rivers in this selfless Oneness, but also to see their differentiated specificity: here is the heart of Dōgen's nature mysticism.

Rūmī lived in the city of Konya, and unlike Francis or Dōgen did not seek refuge in the mountains. Yet his poetry dazzles with nature imagery: the ocean, camels, lions, elephants, roses, the moon, gazelles, donkeys, jasmine, cypress, nightingales and willows, lemons and gardens. In the mystical world of the Sufis, every creature is a living manifestation of Allah's Creation.

This natural world of forms, consisting of earth and air and fire and water, is insubstantial as "sea foam," or "a dream," or "the dust of a passing horse," the Sufis tell us; it is a mere shadow of the world of meanings, of the world of the spirit. The world of nature was created by Allah, the Hidden Treasure, to make Himself known, though in a veiled manner.[43]

Rūmī's nature mysticism consists of tearing aside the veil of the natural world, to glimpse the radiant face of Allah, the Beloved.

The sun, in Rūmī's poems, becomes a symbol for the Divine. "If this sun should become naked and visible, / neither you would remain nor your breast or hem. / The sun through which the whole world is illuminated – / if it would draw slightly closer, the whole world would burn!" Water becomes the Divine Grace or the Divine Essence, or the rain of mercy, a purifying ablution from heaven. Animals, such as the camel, the fox, the pig or goat, and a flamboyant roster of birds, signify spiritual attributes (or lack of them) in humans. The earthly "rosegarden and the sweet basil, different kinds of anemones, / a violet-bed on the dust, and wind, and water, and fire, O heart!" hint at the magnificence of the heavenly garden, and its green leaves in spring herald the Day of Resurrection promised in the Qur'an. The seasonal changes of the garden, from ripening through death to renewal, reflect the passage of the human soul to God.[44]

As a city dweller Rūmī esteems a natural world tended and cultivated. Wildness, for him, flourishes ideally not in the external world of nature but through inner spiritual passions of men and women fervently seeking the Divine. The outer realm of nature offers emblems of that divinity in an urban sanctuary of arbors, flower beds, pruned orchards, and menageries of domesticated animals and ornamental birds. For Rūmī, these tamed, orderly settings often seem to provide safe haven for the wild, chaotic intoxication of spiritual bliss.

Francis, Dōgen, and Rūmī, then, each imbued a type of medieval "nature mysticism" with his own characteristic flavor. In doing so, each gained access to broader understanding—denying not the world, but the narrow self, and discovering thereby a heightened and vivid sense of life.

The Body

Whether the mystical path of the spirit is Christian, Buddhist, or Islamic, struggles and blessings on that path connect intimately with the physical body.

Francis inherited a long tradition of Christian ambivalence about the body: created in the holy image of God, yet prey to lethal temptations of carnality and all the wiles of Satan; a vessel for the shining, eternal spirit, yet made of perishable clay and subject to rot and corruption.

By the time of the Middle Ages, as is well known, it became customary for Christian ascetics to scourge the flesh with mortification and penances. Hungering for God, they starved the obstinate body. Seeking purity, they flailed it and tried to pummel it into submission. Longing for the *mystica mors*, the mystic death-in-life, they harried the body to its breaking point. They identified the body with "lower nature," the swinish ego. They feared and despised its intemperate demands, its snorting lusts and greeds and its evil compulsions. They strove to build spiritual strength by fighting its desires. They struggled to emulate the tortured Christ by suffering on crosses of their own devising: ice baths, hair shirts, self-whippings with chains, extremes of fasting. Dragging the filthy rag of a sinful body through life, encumbered by it, cursed by it, they prayed fervently to God to rid them of it, and they awaited deliverance to heaven.

Unfortunately, Francis was no exception. In this instance he does not seem modern to us; he seems a medieval fanatic. Though he was sufficiently flexible to permit moderation in the penances of his friars, and told them that each must set his own reasonable standard of asceticism, Francis drove "Brother Donkey"—as he called his own body—very hard. He slept on the ground in winter. He refused basic comforts. Thomas of Celano reports that Francis rarely indulged in cooked food, but if someone offered it, he would first sprinkle it with ashes. Early in his saintly career, when as a young man he felt tormented by sexual desires, Francis would "immerse himself in a ditch filled in winter with ice, remaining in it until every seduction of the flesh went away."[45] Not surprisingly, "Brother Donkey" responded over the years by deteriorating into a disease-riddled nag of skin and bones, frail and festering with poxes and sores and chronic pain, and at the very end wheezing and blind.

To his credit, at the end of his life Francis realized his mistake. At the age of forty-three, as he lay sightless and emaciated, wracked with fevers and wounds, he asked forgiveness of his body. "Rejoice, brother body, and forgive me," the bedridden Francis said. "For behold now I gladly fulfill thy desires, and gladly hasten to attend to thy complaints."[46] He began accepting food and medicine—though by then it proved too late.

The drastic austerities of Francis and his scourging of the body were preceded, more than a millennium-and-a-half earlier, by similar measures undertaken by the Indian prince Siddhartha Gautauma, in the years when he lived in a forest with Hindu yogis, before he became the Buddha. Seeking *moksha*, ultimate liberation, Siddhartha starved himself. He brutally chastened his body, as other yogis did. He nearly died. When he came to his senses, he adopted what he called the "Middle Path," the way of moderation, and he began to eat again and to care for his body in a judicious, even-tempered way. After he became the Buddha, he taught this Middle Path to his students. Buddhism has had little use for the extremes of body-punishing asceticism. Accordingly, for Dōgen, the human body does not hinder enlightenment but serves as the very vehicle through which enlightenment occurs.[47]

In this Dōgen contrasted not only with medieval Christians like Francis, but quite consciously with certain traditionalist doctrines of Theravada Buddhists as expressed in some of the ancient Indian sutras, doctrines which, though rejecting physical mortification, could be viewed as considering the body "impure." Some Buddhist sects have practiced contemplating the unsavoriness of bodily organs, secretions, and functions in order to break attachment, or have sat in charnel grounds and meditated on physical decay and death to prompt awareness of impermanence. Dōgen has no interest in this. His emphasis on the body as a means to enlightenment derives from the critical importance he places on *zazen*, the practice of sitting in meditation. *Zazen* is grounded in the body, in its posture, its crossed legs, its hand positions, its aches and pains, its breathing. *Shikantaza*—or the practice of "just sitting"—and enlightenment are one and the same, as Dōgen never tires of explaining; enlightenment is realized at the moment of sitting.

The body is not an isolated physical entity, however. Mind suffuses it, and body suffuses mind. The two combine so inextricably that it is impossible to separate them, and Dōgen in fact often prefers not to speak of the "body," but of the "body-mind." Dōgen emphasizes that the non-duality of body and mind has always been a major principle of Buddhism. Moreover, the body-mind is not discrete from the larger world, but linked with it in constant, fluid interaction. The body-mind is the whole universe. As Dōgen says: "The body-mind in the Buddha-way is grass, trees, tiles, and stones; it is wind, rain, water and fire." And Dōgen again: "Because the body necessarily fills the mind and the mind inevitably penetrates the body, we call this the permeation of body-mind. That is to say, this is the entire world and all directions, the whole body and the whole mind. This is none other than joy of a very special kind."[48]

As the "Heart Sutra" of Mahayana Buddhism proclaims, form is emptiness; the bodily form that our small ego-self takes for granted in our everyday life as a solid, autonomous, and stable entity (despite all evidence to the contrary) in fact is empty of inherent substance. As the "Heart Sutra" also proclaims, however, emptiness is form; the non-substantial and undifferentiated reality of Buddha-nature manifests fully in the forms of our individuated physical bodies, these marvels of flesh in their unique thusness, fleetingly alive within the world of transient phenomena.

In the enlightenment that occurs in the moment of "just sitting," when ego dissolves and the dualism of body and mind is cast off ("To be enlightened by all things of the universe is to cast off the body and mind of the self as well as those of others," Dōgen says[49]) then a realized unity is experienced. Mediated and purified by emptiness and free of self-centered orientation, Kim writes, explaining Dōgen's attitude, the true human body functions in harmony with the entire universe. In summary: "We search with the body, practice with the body, attain enlightenment with the body, and understand with the body."[50]

Rūmī quested with the body, too—a body in service to spirit. Rūmī and other Sufis recognize three levels of existence. These are Allah, the spiritual, and the material. The body, of course, combines two of these levels, as a material entity infused with spirit. Moreover, the perfect body of Adam, and the bodies of all subsequent humans, have been created in the image of Allah. The spirit abides in the transcendent realm of "meanings," in the brilliance of the nine heavenly spheres, but it manifests in this shadowy, earthly realm of "forms"—first as mineral, then as animal, and finally as human. When spirit manifests in a human body, its consciousness is at the bestial level of the ego. But it can acquire virtues by starting to free itself of ego, allowing the spirit to ascend the spiritual ladder toward the liberation of *fanā'* and *baqā'*, and ultimate experience of Allah.[51]

Rūmī comments frequently on the relationship between body and spirit. Sometimes he stresses the yearning of spirit to escape the physical body: "The spirit is like a falcon, the body its fetter—the poor foot-bound, broken-winged creature!" or "When will the bird of my spirit fly from the cage toward the garden?" We should not assume, however, that such statements imply a dichotomy between evil flesh and glorious spirit. In reality, both body—the external manifestation of spirit—and the spirit itself can be wholesome and healthy and good, and function together.[52]

Thus Rūmī emphasizes that the body can reveal the hidden grace of spirit. "The body moves by means of the spirit, but you do not see the spirit: Know the spirit through the body's movement!"[53] This seems a natural sentiment for a man who spun beatifically for hours as a whirling dervish, conveying the bliss of his spirit through the dance of his body.

Like all good Sufis, Rūmī did engage not only in ritual prayer, but in prolonged fasting, certainly during Ramadan and at other times as well. But his fasting never reached the extremes that Francis undertook. It was meant to purify, not punish, the body. Rūmī asserts in the *Mathnawī* that "the spirit cannot function without the body, and the body without the spirit is withered and cold. / Your body is manifest and your spirit is hidden: These two put all the business of the world in order." And again: "God made the body the locus of manifestation for the spirit."[54]

As noted previously in the section on "Love," Rūmī in his poems used bodily imagery with verve and uninhibited delight when describing the seeker's passionate quest for the Divine Beloved. The eyes "sweet and full of fire," the "slender and delicate" lips with their mad kisses, the "beautiful, moon-enslaving Face" and the curve of the eyebrow, the "veils of musky hair," the curls of tresses.[55] As in the Hebrew Bible's Song of Songs, the body in its erotic splendor becomes a celebration of the sacred, a focus for the ardor of the soul as it craves God.

In Francis, Dōgen, and Rūmī, then, we find three distinct medieval attitudes toward the physical body: as an emblem of "lower nature," to be scorned in favor of the higher spirit; as an inseparable element of body-mind, vehicle for enlightenment; and as the outer manifestation of spirit, capable of dancing in passionate joy and longing toward the Divine.

The Role of Women

Whether in the Europe of Francis, or in Dōgen's Japan, or in Rūmī's Anatolia, thirteenth-century women struggled under enormous disadvantages.

In Europe, girls could be married legally at twelve, and most were wed at fourteen or sixteen. The majority, uneducated except in the tasks of routine household drudgery, were then consigned for the rest of their often brief lives to endless pregnancies, which could easily prove fatal.

Believed weaker by nature and ranked near the bottom of the social hierarchy, medieval European women were thought to be in need of protection from husbands, who they were expected to obey in return for receiving shelter, safety, and love. Societies decreed that women required such protection not only from brute male lust, always lurking outside the home, but from their own natural female seductiveness and wanton licentiousness.

In speaking about medieval European women we must differentiate between a noblewoman and a rural peasant and a city woman, and in the latter case between a patrician woman, an artisan's wife, or a female servant.[56] Nevertheless they all shared certain liabilities. Severe restrictions limited their right to inherit property or to manage it. Though medieval women could enter religious life as cloistered nuns, they could not participate in active church leadership. They could not preach. They could not participate officially in the Church. They generally could not hold public office. They did not receive equal rights in courts of law. [57]

In an age of ubiquitous Christian faith, perhaps the most crippling and humiliating disadvantage for European women of the Middle

Ages was the image of the female sex propagated by the Church. Priests reminded them constantly of St. Paul's declaration, in Ephesians, that wives must obey their husbands. Women heard repeatedly, too, from Church fathers that Eve, a secondary creature fashioned from Adam's rib, had in her weakness and foolishness condemned the human race to sin and death by succumbing to the wiles of Satan. The Church identified women with nature, fecund and lovely but often raw and filthy and dangerous and unpredictable, and identified men with higher mind or pure, transcendent spirit.

While demeaned by the Church and deprived of legal rights and social freedom, however, medieval European women also were honored and idealized. Though sinful as Eve, women were also chaste as the Blessed Mother of God, the Holy Virgin Mary. Though frail, deficient, and tempted to wickedness by nature, nevertheless women—especially noblewomen in the age of chivalry and courtly love—were romantically adored, sentimentalized, and worshipped for their purity. It was the traditional sexist dichotomy of Whore and Virgin, and it very effectively trapped women of the era.

Women in medieval Anatolia or in Kamakura-era Japan fared no better than women in the Italy of the Holy Roman Empire. Wives needed to submit always to husbands, the birth of sons was cause for proud rejoicing, and the birth of daughters for disappointment. It seems all the more surprising, therefore, that Francis and Dōgen and Rūmī defied some of the conventional ways of treating women in their societies.

When young Clare of Assisi decided to renounce her privileged life among the aristocracy, wishing to follow Francis as a barefoot wanderer and beggar out in the wild countryside among robbers and rapists and brigands, serving lepers and the poor, she acted with exceptional boldness. Women simply did not do such a thing. If inspired to a religious life, a woman became a nun and joined a cloister to retire from the world. What Clare proposed was unprecedented. Yet Francis did not turn her away.[58]

On the night of Palm Sunday in 1212, in St. Mary's, one of the chapels he had restored with his own hands, Francis met Clare and brazenly cut off her hair, giving her the monk's tonsure—contrary to Church law, because Francis was neither priest nor bishop—then gave her a friar's sackcloth tunic to wear. Francis welcomed her into the protection of the Church. He could not permit her to live with him or his friars, or to walk the hazardous countryside, but he did prepare a sanctuary for her at his chapel of San Damiano, where five years earlier he had heard the voice of Christ. Eventually Clare was joined by several women of her family and by other women steadfastly committed to a life of utmost poverty. It was the start of the Franciscan Order of the Poor Clares.[59]

When Francis, at Clare's request, drafted a document in 1215 outlining a formal rule for the Order and submitted it to Rome, the pope approved it as a special "Privilege of Poverty"—another milestone. For the first time in Church history, women received the right to live as a monastic community devoted to shared material poverty and spiritual liberation through Christ, exactly like Francis and his brethren.[60]

Dōgen, too, pioneered new opportunities for women within his spiritual tradition.

In medieval Japan, Buddhist monasteries maintained secluded areas with a policy of *niyonin-kinzei*, or "no admittance to woman." Dōgen, with his typically forthright sense of independence, mocked this as a "ridiculous custom."[61]

Dōgen trained female monastics, women who left a nunnery in order to study Sōtō Zen with him on an equal footing with men. This is astonishing for medieval Japan, or anywhere in the thirteenth century, for that matter. The first woman to join Dōgen was Ryōnen. Dōgen praised her, saying that she had "peerless aspiration to enlightenment" and was "deeply devoted to the great way of the buddhas"[62]— and Dōgen had extremely high standards. Ryōnen is credited with being the primary influence on one of Dōgen's most straightforward teachings about equality between male and female practitioners, the "Bendōwa" ("On the Endeavor of the Way") section of the *Shōbōgenzō*, written in 1231 as a series of questions and answers regarding Zen practice. In "Question 13" someone asks "Should zazen be practiced by lay men and women?" Dōgen replies that in understanding Buddha dharma there is no distinction between men and women—or between nobles and commoners, for that matter.[63]

Another of Dōgen's female monastics was Eshin, for whom Dōgen performed a ceremony commemorating her father's death. One of Dōgen's most devoted female monastics was Egi, whom he met in the winter of 1234, and who accompanied him and his other students when he moved into the wild mountains of Echizen. Egi studied with Dōgen for twenty years, assisting at his sick bed before he left on his final journey to Kyoto in 1253. Dōgen respected and honored her, and Egi remained a significant figure in the leadership of Dōgen's monastery in the generation after his death.[64]

In addition to the "Bendōwa" question-and-answer section, Dōgen made other explicit references to male and female equality in the *Shōbōgenzō*. In the "Raihai-tokuzui" chapter, or "Receiving the Marrow by Bowing," written in 1240, he expresses a hope that discrimination between men and women will break down, and repeats a famous Ch'an story about a nun, Miaoxin, who was appointed head monastic in a temple. One day she enlightened a group of seventeen male monks by making a deeply insightful comment regarding a *kōan*. Dōgen praises her lavishly by writing that her teaching surpassed anything "the bodhisattvas of three classes or ten stages can come up with."[65]

In the same chapter he also declares:

> Those who are extremely stupid think that women are merely the objects of sexual desire and treat women in this way. The Buddha's children should not be like this. If we discriminate against women because we see them

merely as objects of sexual desire, do we also discriminate against men for the same reason? ....What is the fault of women? What is the virtue of men? There are unwholesome men, and there are wholesome women. Hoping to hear dharma and leave the household does not depend on being female or male. Before becoming free of delusion, men and women are equally not free from delusion. At the time of becoming free from delusion and realizing the truth, there is no difference between men and women.[66]

Obviously, as a statement made in the thirteenth century, this is far ahead of its time. The same cannot entirely be said for several of Rūmī's statements, however. Although Rūmī often professes sincere and glowing admiration for women, nevertheless in the *Mathnawī* he also writes: "Know that your ego is indeed a woman—it is worse than a woman, for the woman is a part of evil, your ego the whole." And: "The superiority of men over women—oh worshipper of the present!— is that men see better the ends of things." In the *Fihi ma fihi*: "Women are for children and satisfying passion." In the *Dīvān-e*: "By the spirit of all Men! Whoever is not a lover of God is a woman in meaning— behold then what sort of women are women!" And: "Woman is she whose way and goal are color and scent: She is the reality of the ego that commands to evil...." And this: "Join us like a man, for you are a lion! Why do you let your heart flutter like a woman?" And also this: "Jump up, let us dance, clapping our hands! For we have been delivered from women through our manliness!" And finally: "Existence is for women—the work of men is nonexistence. Thanks be to God, for we have risen as champions in nonexistence!"[67]

Rūmī also sometimes personifies the Divine Beloved as a cunning female: "She whose beautiful face makes man her slave....She whose haughtiness causes your heart to tremble....She whose disdain fills your heart and soul with blood...."[68]

Granted, in these verses Rūmī employs common Sufi symbolism. The intellect is viewed as male and heavenly, the ego as female and earthly. Chittick explains that "Rūmī 's verses often follow the symbolism of this cosmological scheme, so that 'men' are symbols of the saints and 'women' are the symbols of the unbelievers." But in this symbolism, "men" and "women" also can stand for spiritual qualities not exclusive to gender. As Chittick elaborates, a person—whether male or female—who is dominated by intellect would be symbolized, in Rūmī 's poems, by the term "men"; a person—whether female or male—who is dominated by ego would be symbolized by the term "women." Thus, a defender of Rūmī 's symbolism might argue that although his verses may seem misogynistic, in reality the evil "women" they designate could refer to ego-dominated men. The valiant "men" they refer to could apply to women of intellect. Additionally, says Chittick, when Rūmī employs feminine references to describe the Divine Beloved, he transforms the "negative" view of women to "positive," because now the feminine "reflects and displays God's Beauty, Gentleness, and Mercy."[69]

Further, as other scholars point out in Rūmī 's defense, his work accords with a Sufi system in which both *nafs*, or ego, and *Dhāt*, or Divine Essence, are represented as female, so that the spiritual seeker is depicted as moving between two poles, from an inferior feminine to an exalted feminine.[70]

The *nafs/Dhāt* polarity, however, simply seems like the medieval Whore and Virgin dichotomy in yet another guise. Ultimately Rūmī 's relationship to women in his writing remains complicated and troubling. Even if examples of his apparently misogynistic verses represent only a small fraction of statements in the vast corpus of his work, and even if they remain counterbalanced by his validation of women, and even if his Sufi symbolism, when interpreted correctly, grants the possibility of intellect and spiritual virtue to individual, exceptional women, the rhetoric employed by Rūmī in his most disturbing verses is typical of that disdain for women as a group that mars the Middle Ages and is so repugnant in its sexism. At first it might seem possible to defend Rūmī by claiming that he simply was a man of his time. The answer to that claim is: look at Dōgen.

A redeeming feature of Rūmī 's attitude toward women is that he did teach female disciples, and some of those women became very accomplished Sufi adepts themselves. This was in keeping with the tradition of the famed eighth-century female Sufi saint, Rabi'a al-'Adawiyya, and other Sufi women who endeavored to perfect themselves on the path of *tariqa*. Rūmī took the spirituality of his own women disciples very seriously, and his letters to them glow with warmth.

We also should note that Rūmī's first mother-in-law was a distinguished Sufi adept, considered by many his spiritual equal. Additionally, Rūmī's favorite female disciple, Fateme Khatun, married Rūmī's oldest son, and their daughters—treasured by Rūmī—grew to become women regarded in Konya as saints who produced miracles and offered spiritual teachings to other women.[71] In this regard Rūmī deserves praise.

Spiritual Retreat and Social Engagement

Many people who commit themselves to a life of spiritual illumination must face, eventually, three choices: whether to balance personal retreats with involvement in conventional society; whether to renounce mainstream society and join a new and more secluded one of fellow seekers; or whether to withdraw altogether into solitary hermitage. Rūmī, Francis, and Dōgen each faced these choices, and each made a decision that dramatically shaped his life.

Rūmī lacked the option of monasticism, which would have allowed him to become part of an isolated community of like-minded spiritual practitioners. In contrast to Buddhism, with its history of monks' *avasas,* or retreat communities, in India dating to the fifth century BCE; in contrast to Judaism, with its history of Essene monks living at Qumram in the first century CE; and in contrast to Christianity, which saw its first monasteries emerge in the Egyptian desert in the fourth century CE, Islam has no monastic tradition. In fact, because Muslims esteem marriage as a crucial part of religious life, Islam generally does not esteem celibacy or monasticism as praiseworthy. Moreover, because Sufis see the world as radiating the divine Presence of God, they do not withdraw from it into monastic life. And finally, although early Sufis embraced asceticism, Sufi mystics disdained it except as a preparatory and peripheral means to the goal of realizing extinction of the ego in God, because asceticism relies solely on an act of will rather than an act of submission.[72] Therefore Rūmī chose to balance spiritual retreats, or *khalwa,* with living in the world.

Before he met Shams, Rūmī engaged the world of Konya as family man and respected Sufi scholar, Islamic legal expert, and preacher; after his fateful meeting with the "Sun of Tabriz" he encountered his city differently, as a singer of verses and a twirling street dancer. But he still gave *fatwās,* or legal decisions, sometimes even while dancing. He remained vibrantly alive to the city and available to it. Rūmī dined with wealthy friends, he strolled the bazaars with his companion Hosamoddin while dictating the reeling verses of the *Mathnawī,* he lolled in the baths, he dawdled with shopkeepers and chatted with children and listened to the flutes and stringed instruments of all-night *samā*̄ parties. These experiences fed his lilting, exuberant poetry. Yet Rūmī also could adopt in *khalwa,* long periods of fasting and prayer, a secluded existence that facilitated deeper connection with the Divine Presence of God. Frequently, he went on retreat and led a life of withdrawal and contemplation.[73]

For Francis and for Dōgen the option of the monastery did exist, and each made contrasting decisions: Francis adamantly resisted monastic life, virtually as a matter of moral principle, while Dōgen embraced it.

When Francis first hiked barefoot to Rome to meet the highest officials of the Church to inform them that he wished to gather a band of wandering mendicant friars, a cardinal advised him to join a monastery instead. Francis refused.[74] He wanted to live like Jesus, not like a monk.

Many European monasteries of the Middle Ages were essentially country manors endowed by aristocrats to give their noble families a private sanctuary for prayer and lodging, to enhance their standing with the Church, and to increase their chances for eternal salvation. They accepted as monks only the learned and the rich. The wealthy monasteries of the Cluniacs and Cistercians had long been known as pleasure spas for monks who adorned themselves in gorgeous habits made of knights' raiments, lounged in plush beds, and dined with silver spoons.[75]

Francis shunned this. Of course in the end the Church forced him to turn his loose bunch of ragtag friars into an official Order of monks. In the beginning, though, Franciscans opposed monasticism; Francis himself—increasingly alone as the Franciscans grew in his lifetime to an international Order of more than five thousand friars—remained anti-monastic to his final day on earth.[76] He always wished to keep his mission simple: live in poverty, go to the people in the towns, and speak to them in their own language. While simple, it also proved revolutionary. Francis also, like Rūmī, frequently sought spiritual nourishment in reclusive periods of intense, solitary prayer and fasting, forsaking society to commune with God.

Dōgen shared impulses similar to Francis's. "His religion was through and through the religion of the people," declares Kim[77]—although Dōgen did not go out to them, as Francis did. Instead he invited the people, the ones sincerely committed to seeking the Buddha Way, to come to him.

Dōgen, too, like Francis, shunned the monasteries of his day—smug institutions, amassing property and riches, catering to the gentry of Kamakura Japan, keeping armed monks, squabbling among themselves, their Buddhism ritualized and lifeless. But unlike Francis, Dōgen chose a different solution. When he retreated from Kyoto to the wilderness of Echizen in 1243, he started a reformist monastery of his own, focused on *zazen* meditation. He wished to create an ideal community.[78]

He modeled his "Temple of Eternal Peace," hidden among the forests of the far mountains, on the classic Ch'an monasteries of China that he so admired. Like any utopian with the power to achieve his vision, Dōgen left little to chance. He wrote regulations governing meal etiquette, bathing, toothbrushing, the wearing of robes, how to cook the rice. He did this not to micromanage every detail of his monk's lives, not to tyrannize them, but to ensure that things finally were being done properly in a Japanese Buddhist monastery. He did it, too, so that his monastics would learn to exemplify Buddha-nature and to live the precepts through everyday activities. He also did it as a way of encouraging people to perform tasks mindfully, to lead a ritual life in sacred time. He did it so they would realize that nothing is trivial, that even washing hands and faces is sacred liturgy. And most important, he did it to provide a firm structure in which people could experience freedom.[79]

It was a radical experiment, every bit as radical as the one enacted by Francis.

Dōgen challenged his contemporaries—especially other Buddhist monastics—by saying, in effect, "See? This is how people can live together. This is what is possible." He created the Temple of Eternal Peace not to banish himself, but to demonstrate to the world that devoted men and women indeed could flourish in sacred community.

* * *

Francis of Assisi and Dōgen and Rūmī engaged their era and their societies in unique ways. Working without knowledge of one another, in northern Italy and Japan and Anatolia, sometimes their methods and ideas happened to be in accord; sometimes they diverged. In each case, however, the three mystical teachers responded with a level of commitment and zest that attracts people at the start of the twenty-first century.

As we see in the following chapter, this attraction also helps to ensure that new generations continue to discover the Christian saint, the Zen monk, and the Sufi teacher—particularly in the vibrant legacy of their poems.

Chapter Three

The Poetic Works: A Brief Comparative Survey

Francis, Rūmī, and Dōgen were not only mystics and spiritual teachers. They were writers. Or, strictly speaking, Dōgen was a writer, in the sense that we use the term today; he thought of himself as such, drafting and revising poems (and the brilliant dharma talks and philosophical treatises of the *Shōbōgenzō*) specifically for a readership. Rūmī was different. He was a prolific and extraordinarily gifted poet, but he does not seem to have sat down often as a "writer" and composed. Instead, verses simply bubbled out of him; when he wandered in a state of happy inspiration, chirping stanzas, his disciples hurriedly jotted them down. As for Francis, with his skimpy education, he barely wrote anything at all. But he loved to sing. Sometimes he asked a friar to permanently record in writing the verses he created.

As a result we have classic literature from each of the three men, poetic works still popular today. Francis composed one of the first, and most enduring, poems to appear in vernacular Italian. Dōgen authored classic Zen poems. Rūmī contributed to world literature thousands of poems, many of them newly revealed to, and newly beloved by, readers in the West.

The poems of Francis, Dōgen, and Rūmī also give us the direct flavor of these spiritual teachers, a sense of who they were, of what they saw and heard and felt. Otherwise we have little immediate access to their lives. Francis left several official documents, such as the "Rule of 1223" for the Franciscan Order, but to glimpse him, to witness him in action, we may need to turn with some reluctance to the hagiographic accounts—colorfully embellished, and very pious—by those who knew and remembered him, such as Thomas of Celano and Brother Angelo. We may also turn, with even greater reluctance, to those who gained their information second-hand, through interviews, such as Bonaventure and Brother Ugolino, author of the biographical *Little Flowers*. As for Dōgen, he scatters autobiographical snippets throughout the *Shobogenzo* and in some of the dharma hall discourses of his *Eihei Kōroku* compilation, but otherwise we have little first-hand information. With the rise of the Rinzai Zen school in the cities and in the powerful court of the Japanese imperial palace, and the relegation of Dōgen's Sōtō Zen school to the rural hinterlands, he fell into obscurity, largely forgotten for seven hundred years. A biography written by a Sōtō monk named Kenzei was written two hundred years after Dōgen's death, and was augmented in the eighteenth century by another Sōtō monk, Menzan; these secondary sources have provided most of the information we have. Regarding Rūmī, we have recollections passed on by admirers and disciples, and nearly 150 of his letters, saved by one of his sons, who also authored an interpretive biography, but we have no attempt by the *Mawlānā*, or "Master," to chronicle events himself.[1] Thus if we wish to hear the personal lives of Francis, Dōgen, and Rūmī most intimately, in their own voices, we turn to their poems.

What follows is, by necessity, a brief overview of an immense topic. This introduction is offered with hope that it will inspire readers to seek out and savor published collections of the poems, embarking on further explorations of spiritual themes and imagery in the work of these three gifted poets.

"The Canticle of Brother Sun," the most famous verses devised by Francis (he invented a melody for them, too, but it vanished centuries ago), was composed not in High Latin but in everyday language of people living around Assisi. It is the earliest surviving religious poem in Italian. Its use of ordinary speech, with its rolling syllables, is tenderly musical even to a reader who comprehends very little Italian: "*Laudato si, mi signore, per sora luna e le stelle, / in celu l'ai formate clarite et pretiose et belle.*" "Praised be you, My Lord, through Sister Moon and the stars, / in heaven you formed them shining and precious and beautiful."[2]

As scholars have pointed out, and as may be gathered from those two brief lines, most of the verses praise God through ("per") and with ("cun") his creations: "The airy skies," in the words of Francis, "so cloudy and serene." Sister Water, "so necessary, yet so humble and precious, and chaste." Brother Fire, "who lights up the night, / He is beautiful and carefree, robust and fierce." Our sister, Mother Earth, "who nourishes and watches us / While bringing forth abundance of fruits with colored flowers and herbs." Francis also sings praises to God of "those who pardon through your love," and of Sister Death, "whom no living man can escape."[3] In our own time Pope Francis quotes what he calls this "beautiful canticle" in the opening paragraph of his encyclical *Laudato Si'*, and adds, "Saint Francis of Assisi reminds us that our common home is like a sister with whom we share our life" and "a mother who opens her arms to embrace us."[4]

Bernard McGinn, in his history of Western mysticism, notes that Francis was influenced by psalms of creation and the canticles in the Hebrew Bible. Yet the song of Francis "strikes a new note because of the solidarity it expresses between the human and the cosmic order" and because "it conveys an experience of the world as a single harmonious theophany of God." In the "Canticle," McGinn says, "God's presence is experienced as luminously real in the cosmos as a whole and in each of its elements." Indeed, he concludes, these brief verses composed by Francis usher in a new and distinctive form of nature mysticism.[5]

The poems of Rūmī and those of Dōgen present clear contrasts to one another. Rūmī creates with exuberance, in a headlong, gushing effusion of images and rapturous lyricism. In its sensual lushness his poetry resembles the biblical Song of Songs, while its spirit of openhearted invitation leaps centuries ahead and hearkens toward Whitman, and its love of the tangible—lemons, parrots, rubies—presages the work of Neruda.

Dōgen, by comparison, writes terse poems. They are sober and contemplative. In their brevity and compression they anticipate Dickinson (though lacking, in English translation, her electrifying intensity). In their mannered eloquence they seem, always, distinctly Japanese.

Yet despite differences the poems of Rūmī and Dōgen share thematic concerns: loneliness and loss, language and silence, impermanence, and sometimes a preoccupation with specific images, such as a drifting boat or the moon. Most important, they share a fascination with self-abeyance, with the mystical experience of stilling and quieting ego to realize the Absolute. As Sufi master and Zen adept, Rūmī and Dōgen continually explore the act of casting off the small self—the enlightenment experience of *fanā'* in Persian, or *satori* in Japanese—in both their spiritual practices and their poems.

The Sufi poet and the Zen poet left a corpus of inspired work recognized today as exceptionally accomplished and significant.

Rūmī, influenced by the mystic Sufi poets Sanā'ī and 'Aṭṭār, produced more than 35,000 lyrical verses, including those collected in the *Rubaiyat* quatrains, the *Dīwān-e Shams-e Tabrīzī*, and the *Mathnawī*.[6] Fresh, contemporary translations from the original Persian make his work accessible and engaging to modern American readers.

Dōgen, too, enjoys exalted status, if not among the popular reading public then certainly among the growing and enthusiastic legions of Buddhist followers in the West. While his reputation as a leading writer and thinker derives primarily from the prose work of the *Shōbōgenzō*, his poems, influenced by the Ch'an poet Hongzhi and others, remain highly esteemed both within his home country and abroad. This is particularly so since 1968, when they were highlighted in Kawabata Yasunari's Nobel Prize acceptance speech.[7]

In approaching the poems of Rūmī and Dōgen it helps if we investigate commonalities of theme and imagery. The theme of loneliness and loss, referred to above, permeates some of Rūmī's most powerful poems, created in the immediate aftermath of the loss of his revered Shams. It also tinges many of Dōgen's verses. For Rūmī, the separation from Shams symbolizes the soul's agonizing estrangement from Allah. [8] Consider this excerpt of a poem from the *Dīwān-e*:

> In separation, the lover is like a name empty of meaning;
> > but a meaning such as belovedness has no need of
> > names.
> You are the sea, I am a fish – hold me as you desire;
> > show compassion, exercise kingly power – without you,
> > I remain alone . . .
> Without you, the world is a torment; may it not be
> > without you for a single instant; by your life I implore
> > this, for life without you is a torture and an agony to
> > me . . . .
> > Exalted be God, exalted be God! . . .[9]

In opening lines of another poem in the *Dīwān-e*, Rūmī writes: "Since you deserted me death is for me joy and ease; without / you death has become for me like honey and milk."[10] Dōgen, too, uses images "usually associated with poetic feelings of loss and loneliness to express his religious views or personal experiences," according to Steven Heine, in a critical study that accompanies *The Zen Poetry of Dōgen*:

Genuine spiritual realization must be found by embracing—rather than eliminating—one's emotional response to variability and inevitable loss. The poignantly moved heart (*kokoro*) which feels 'sadness' (*aijaku*) and 'dismay' (*kiken*) undergoes a feeling of turmoil and anguish in the face of change. This level of awareness is crucial for stirring the mind to pursue enlightenment because it discloses an overriding moral impulse to terminate the suffering of self and others based on an underlying identification with the ephemeral fate of all natural phenomena.[11]

Whereas Rūmī issues a passionate cry of grief at feeling separated from the Beloved, Dōgen offers a wistful poem of reflection, a feeling of longing and melancholy prompted by his separation from "home." This is both the literal home and the symbolic "true home" of Zen, which is enlightened Original Nature:

All last night and
This morning still,
Snow falling in the deepest mountains;
Ah, to see the autumn leaves
Scattering in my home.[12]

Rūmī and Dōgen share, too, a concern with issues of language and silence. Mystical experience consists of moments of heightened clarity that often, to the person experiencing them, feel ineffable. If words and rational concepts seem redundant, or misleading, or inadequate at such moments, the best response can be to remain silent. In his poem "Moses and the Shepherd" Rūmī imagines God speaking to Moses:

That broken-open lowliness is the reality,
not the language! Forget phraseology.
I want burning, *burning*.[13]

Rūmī wants burning, too, the blazing of *fanā*, the inferno that annihilates selfish ego and leaves the soul clean and pure for its experience of *baqā*, of abiding in God. If language becomes an impediment to *fanā*, what can a poet do? An option is to renounce poetry altogether. Rūmī once remarked, "By Allah, I care nothing for poetry, and there is nothing worse in my eyes than that."[14] As Annemarie Schimmel explains in her study of Rūmī, he also may have said this because he wished to indemnify himself against a Qur'anic condemnation of hypocritical poets, and those poets who taint themselves by writing religiously forbidden songs of love and wine.[15] However, if the primary reason for his assertion was that, as a mystic, he felt impeded by language, yet another option was to abandon not merely poetry but all speaking and writing, favoring silence:

> Go through the ear to the center
> where sky is, where wind,
> where silent knowing.[16]

And again:

> Be silent! Be silent! for love behaves contrary to normal;
> Here the meaning hides itself if you talk too much. [17]

Rūmī, according to Fatemeh Keshavarz in *Reading Mystical Lyric: The Case of Jalāl al-Dīn Rumi,* invokes silence for many reasons: because it can circumvent the garrulous intellect; or because silence is the realm in which the unexpected manifests itself; or because it can liberate us from fixed means of expression; or because the Divine commands a seeker to maintain silence, preventing disclosure of spiritual secrets; or simply because "the only true 'house of God' is love itself," which is "indescribable."[18] (Invoking Julia Kristeva's *Revolution in Poetic Language*, we also might propose that in invoking silence Rūmī—and Dōgen —go beyond signification and the semiotic in a return to the pre-verbal.)[19] Yet again and again Rūmī returns to language, to poetry remarkable for its fervor and rapt, luxuriant sensuality.

Dōgen, like Rūmī, feels ambivalent about language. Compared to the importance of *zazen* meditation and following the Buddha way, he declares in the *Shōbōgenzō*, "the composition of literature, Chinese poetry and Japanese verse is worthless, and it must be renounced."[20] This should come as no surprise, as Zen often eschews the verbal and abstract in favor of the hands-on and empirical. Zen is "a special transmission outside the scriptures," as the legendary Zen ancestor Bodhidharma is said to have proclaimed, "no dependence upon words and letters; direct pointing to the heart...; seeing into one's own nature."

Dōgen composed a poem on this theme, entitled "No reliance on words and letters":

> Not limited
> By language,
> It is ceaselessly expressed;
> So, too, the way of letters
> Can display but not exhaust it.[21]

"It" in the poem is Buddha nature, or True Nature, or dharma. The paradox, of course, is that Dōgen uses a poem—a highly contrived artifact of language—to express awareness of the limitations of language. While he and Rūmī, gifted poets, sometimes profess an attitude of mistrust toward poetry, toward language itself they move in a relationship of dynamic tension, aware of its constraints yet celebrating its richness. Dōgen responds to a traditional Zen charge that words and images are "painted rice cakes," mere illusions, by affirming that "painted rice cakes" can satisfy hunger.[22] Moreover, he insists that active expression in its full exertion—whether wordless or through a linguistic symbol—directly manifests Buddha-nature; he calls it "intimate language."[23] Thus, although he urges caution in the uncritical use of words, Dōgen performs his own poetic labors in earnest, crafting his Zen verses with precision and care. And Rūmī, though he sometimes disavows language, obviously revels in it. He basks in the sonorities of medieval Persian, delights in his mastery of its meters and techniques, and often sports with words in a festive mood of buoyancy and joy. Moreover, Rūmī is capable of transforming language in a way that mirrors the inner transformation of the exalted Sufi who seeks God, as Keshavarz explains. Rūmī's poems "provide examples of the linguistic transformation of the dirge of referential language into the whirling dance of poetry . . . these poems are nothing if not textualizations of the mystical changes within. They are the experience itself."[24]

Keshavarz further notes that many of Rūmī's poems also textualize the experience of ephemerality—creating an outer world of wildly shifting surfaces and a reeling inner world of spiritual mutability. Transience dominates Rūmī's poems, as objects and identities switch or disappear or return in new guises, refusing to stay fixed or permanent. In a poem from the *Dīwān-e*, dust becomes a jewel; dry land becomes a river; gallows become pulpits.[25] In another poem "the four elements are in fervor":

> Neither is the fire still nor the earth nor the air.
> Sometimes the earth slips into the garb of a plant;
> Sometimes water turns into air because of love.
> The water in oil turns into fire, then fire turns into air
>   similarly because of love.[26]

Dōgen, too, addresses the theme of ephemerality, but while Rūmī does so by presenting a giddy series of metamorphoses in a world of ceaseless flux, Dōgen offers a quiet, sensitive view of impermanence:

> Dewdrops on a blade of grass,
> Having so little time

Before the sun rises;
Let not the autumn wind
Blow so quickly on the field.[27]

Heine comments:

Here the dew epitomizes the fleeting quality of all things....
The aim in expressing a metaphysical understanding of
impermanence...is to send an implicit moral message....
People, who are subject to the same laws that govern the
dew, must seize the opportunity to take advantage of the
fleeting but complete here-and-now moments that recur
in the inevitable movement from life to death.[28]

Rūmī and Dōgen also share specific images, referring frequently to
the moon and—in keeping with their interest in ego-abeyance—to the
self as an unmoored boat. As an example of the latter, Rūmī describes
the arduous struggle of the self, the "helpless little boat," in the throes
of its existential travail and its hazardous journey toward God:

Many ships were wrecked in this storm;
What is my little helpless boat in comparison?

The waves destroyed my ship, neither good remained nor
  bad;
Free from myself, I tied my body to a raft.
Now, I am neither up nor down – no this is not a fair
  description;
I am up on a wave one instant, and down under another
  the next.
I am not aware of my existence, I know only this:
When I am, I am not, and when I am not, I am![29]

This harrowing symbolic depiction of the self battered and helpless and "lost at sea" ends with a triumphant realization of *fanā'* ("Free from myself. . . I am not aware of my existence . . . when I am not, I am!"). Compare this to Dōgen's Zen poem:

> In the heart of the night,
> The moonlight framing
> A small boat drifting,
> Tossed not by the waves
> Nor swayed by the breeze.[30]

Rūmī's boat poem describes the challenges of the self, buffeted and destroyed by storms and thus liberated, riding each cresting wave; Dōgen's boat poem describes a different attainment of enlightenment, in which the boat remains serenely unperturbed by waves and breezes. In Rūmī's poem, Keshavarz writes, the poet is passionately engaged in struggle, "caught in the storm instead of commenting on it with aloofness."[31] For Heine, however, reading Dōgen's poem, aloofness is the salient quality: the boat poem suggests Dōgen's "personal sense of aloofness" as well as "an aesthetic state of solitude" and the "doctrine of casting off-body-mind." The boat has been "transformed here into a symbol of the strength, detachment and dedication required in the search for enlightenment."[32]

Rūmī and Dōgen often utilize imagery of the moon as well. Rūmī's references are far too numerous to cite in their entirety; a few representative ones, chosen at random, include (from quatrains in the *Rubaiyat*) "Those of you in the nightsky above the moon, / try walking damp ground"; "Gone, inner and outer / no moon, no ground or sky"; and (from the *Dīwān-e*), "shine in the window of the soul like the moon from above"; "When your fantasy shines on me like the moon at the full"; and "Moon, have you seen His face and stolen beauty from Him?" The meaning of the moon for Rūmī changes depending on the poetic context, assert both Chittick and Schimmel; Keshavarz agrees, writing that the "moon . . .journeying 'footless' and brave in 'nothingness'" in one poem becomes a "powerless, isolated lover" in another poem and "melts away in the dark night of love. In another instance . . . the moon . . . represents the radiant face of the beloved":[33]

> The heaven and earth are but mirrors;
> The moon of your face reflected in them.
> The mirror has come to life with the reflection;
> To catch a glimpse of the beauty.[34]

Compare this with Dōgen:

> The moon mirrored
> By a mind free
> Of all distractions;
> Even the waves, breaking,
> Are reflecting its light.[35]

In Rūmī's poem, the cosmos reflects the radiance of God; in Dōgen's, the enlightened mind reflects the radiance of the cosmos.

Dōgen's numerous references to the moon in other poems range from the anecdotal and naturalistic to, again, the spiritually symbolic. "The image of illumination by the moon," writes Heine, "has connotations from the poetic tradition, in which it represents an object of longing and the source of comfort in times of turmoil and grief, as well as Buddhist implications" as a symbol of enlightenment, of the "universal manifestations of the compassion and wisdom of Buddha-nature." Examples of the "naturalistic moon" include (from Dōgen's *Eihei Kōroku* collection), "In the sky at dawn / There is only the round, pale moon"; "as the snow even conceals the moon and clouds"; "the moon / Beyond the peak / Is not my companion on this hill"; and the profoundly affecting lines at the beginning of the poem Dōgen penned two weeks before his death: "Just when my longing to see / The moon over Kyoto / One last time grows deepest . . . ." Examples of the "spiritually symbolic moon" of enlightenment include "In the dead of the night, / the moon low in the sky, / As Sakyamuni [the Buddha] enters parinirvana [complete enlightenment]"; and (in Dōgen's "Poems From the Grass Hut" collection), "Contemplating the clear moon / Reflecting a mind empty as the open sky . . . ."[36] There is also the poem called "Direct Mind Seeing the Moon, Sixteenth Night":

> Contemplate on the sixteenth-night koan.
> When body moon tries for fullness, mind moon starts to
>   fade.
> If you have a clear idea of moon, a moon will be born.
> But how can mid-autumn moon be grasped? [37]

This poem is itself a kōan, pointing to the process of enlightenment. In *Moon in a Dewdrop: Writings of Zen Master Dōgen*, Kazuaki Tanahashi notes that Dōgen also uses the image of moonlight shimmering in a droplet of dew, employing it "to describe the state of meditation." Dōgen "suggests that just as the entire moon is reflected in a dewdrop, a complete awakening of truth can be experienced by the individual human being."[38]

Self-Abeyance

In his poem "The Praise of the Virtues," probably composed in Assisi after 1220, Francis declares:

> May the Lord protect all of you holy virtues, for you
>   found your source in him and come forth from Him.
> No man in this world can possess you if he does not die
>   to self. [39]

This dying to self, of course, is the experience Dōgen knew as *satori* and Rūmī knew as *fanā'*—moments of extinguishing the "small self," seeing with dazzling clarity the vast, manifold reality of the universe as well as feeling it, directly and intimately, in a state of inseparable Wholeness.

Dōgen's Zen poems of self-abeyance, notable for their brevity and delicacy, are rooted in Japanese aesthetic ideals of *sabi*, tranquility; *yūgen*, an ambiance of subtle, brooding mystery; and *aware*, or poignancy.[40] His poems of self-transcendence emerge from a state of placid contemplation:

> Just at the moment
> Ear and sound
> Do not interfere –
> There is no voice;
> There is no speaker.[41]

The moment of no interference, of "no voice" and "no speaker," of no interceding "I" to process and organize information, is the moment of *satori*. It is the moment of Francis's dying to self, the moment of simple being, when body and mind have dropped away; the moment of open awareness.

> Long night,
> Long as the
> Long tail of the pheasant:
> The light of dawn
> Breaking through.[42]

The "light of dawn / Breaking through," of course, also represents *satori*. A Dōgen poem called "The Point of Zazen" concludes with these lines, evoking the clarity of supreme awareness:

Realization, neither general nor particular,
is effort without desire.
Clear water all the way to the bottom;
a fish swims like a fish.
Vast sky transparent throughout;
a bird flies like a bird.[43]

If Dōgen's Zen poems of self-abeyance function through nuance, subtle shadings, and restraint, the Sufi poems of self-abeyance composed by Rūmī sprawl across the page in delirious outpourings of anguish and euphoria, the sublime ravings of a soul besotted by its visions of the abrupt unveiling of God:

O lovers, lovers, the time of union and encounter has
    come. The proclamation from heaven has come:
    "Moon-faced beauties, welcome hither!"
Joyous hearts, joyous hearts, joy has come skirt a-trailing;
    we have seized its chain, it has seized our skirts . . .
The seven spheres of heaven are drunk with passion for
    you . . . .[44]

And this:

Like the rose I am laughing with all my body, not only
    with my mouth, because I am without myself, alone
    with the king of the world.
You who came with torch and at dawn ravished my heart,
    dispatch my soul after my heart, do not seize my heart
    alone . . . .[45]

"I am without myself" is Rūmī's ecstatic shout of ego-suspension. And again:

> Today give in full measure that pure wine; strike in utter
> confusion this hasty wheel of heaven. . .
> Love, whose trade is joy, sweet of speech and sweet of
> thought, snatch now the veil from the face of that
> veiled king . . . .[46]

The "veiled king," obviously, is God. And this:

> I beheld the lovely rosebower face, that eye and lamp of
> all brightness,
> That altar before which the soul prostrates, that gladness
> and place of security.
> The heart said, "I will yield up my soul there, I will let go
> of being and selfhood."
> The soul also joined in the concert and began to clap
> hands . . . .[47]

And finally this:

> . . . I became drunken, I became full of enchantment.
> He said: you are a little too intelligent! affected with fancy
> and disbelief;
> I became foolish, I became ignorant, I freed myself of
> all.[48]

To have "freed myself of all" is the goal of mystical spiritual practice.

In their poems of self-abeyance, Francis and Dōgen and Rūmī gave voice to their experience of having "freed myself of all," and in doing so they help readers today to savor the taste of Christian illumination, of Zen *satori*, of Sufi *fanā'* and *baqā'*—the taste of liberation.

As we see in the following chapter, that liberation is the essence of the mystic's journey.

Chapter Four

What Francis, Dōgen, and Rūmī Offer Spiritual Seekers Today

Through making their mystical realizations come alive in the world—a turbulent one, much like the world we recognize today—Francis, Dōgen, and Rūmī show us how we, too, might transform ourselves and our surroundings and how we, too, might open to awareness of the sacred.

We might do it by becoming virtuosic spiritual practitioners, as they did, fully devoted in waking ourselves to God or to Buddhanature or to another realization of the Absolute. Or we may practice at more modest spiritual levels. Most of us will, in fact, grow more modestly. Either way, we can learn from the varied practices, styles, and strategies of Francis and Dōgen and Rūmī, three enlightened contemporaries of the Middle Ages. Without idolizing or revering them, we can embrace them as spiritual friends and mentors.

We can learn to live the everyday astonishment of this sacred world. They show us how.

* * *

Today we find that Francis has become the eponym and hero of a widely admired pope; Dōgen, one of the most quoted and influential Zen teachers in the world; and Rūmī more popular than ever among people of many spiritual traditions. When we began our exploration of Francis, Dōgen, and Rūmī and the era in which they lived, we asked: What accounts for the enduring popularity of these three mystics? And why do they matter to us today? Now, having made their acquaintance further, we can answer:

They serve as exemplars of spiritual courage. Called to spiritual life, they met hardships through both perseverance of will and surrender of self, and throughout they maintained trust in their vocation, in their deepest purpose. They never gave up. Their spiritual courage allowed them to withstand challenges, losses, and doubts; it gave them stamina to endure arduous physical tests of lengthy Christian prayer retreat or Zen *sesshin* or Sufi *khalwa*; their courage sustained them in venturing into new lands, whether Egypt or China or Anatolia, and in launching new endeavors, whether founding new Orders or building a new sanctuary; most of all their spiritual courage endowed them with bold vision, a willingness to dare, an ability to go beyond what others settle for, beyond comfort, beyond the familiar, and risk all in seeking authentic spiritual life at the Source. We can look to Francis, Dōgen, and Rūmī today for inspiration in our own quests.

They also demonstrate possibilities for dramatic personal change. As we have seen, the Italian playboy who became a saint, the young Japanese aristocrat who became a reformist monk, and the Anatolian lawyer who became an ecstatic poet show us that we need not remain stuck in our social roles, in our personal quagmires. We can transform. We can wrest free. We can become the person we are most deeply called to be. Francis, Dōgen, and Rūmī can serve as models, and we can appreciate each of these teachers for the distinctive characteristics he developed from his training: Rūmī for his ardor and trenchant insights; Dōgen for his intellectual acumen and innovation; Francis for his simplicity and beneficence.

Moreover, these spiritual seekers prove to us that we can find our own way. Steeped in their religious traditions, and esteeming those traditions highly, nevertheless when their contemporaries offered them little of value Francis, Dōgen, and Rūmī devised new approaches, new ideas and practices, that opened new pathways of spiritual fulfillment while enlivening the traditions they loved. Francis, Dōgen, and Rūmī did what they needed to do—whatever it took, whatever the personal cost—to accomplish what their innermost voice told them was most urgent, most vital. While preserving what was essential and alive in their religions, they discarded shopworn pieties, abandoned dogma, and defied convention. Their power lay in not caring what others thought. Their power lay in confidence and independence. They did not fit in, so they created what they needed—and what their traditions needed. They found their own spiritual paths, and show us that we can, too.

As we also have seen, this trio of thirteenth-century teachers remains pertinent because they feel modern to us. Unlike many of their medieval contemporaries, who often seem stodgy and antiquated, and who mostly are forgotten, Francis and Dōgen and Rūmī feel familiar and alive. We recognize their concerns, their thoughts, their voices.

For example, their efforts to find viable roles for women in religious society feel meaningful to us. In countless churches, temples, and mosques today, women still struggle for parity with men. As we have noted, the theme of women and their proper role in religious society engaged Francis, Dōgen, and Rūmī and, unlike many of their contemporaries, the three mystical teachers found ways to include women.

In thirteenth-century Italy, Japan, and Anatolia and throughout the medieval world, women struggled under oppressive patriarchal conditions. As we have seen, Francis defied convention by accepting

Clare into his Order, cutting her hair in the monk's tonsure and giving her the sackcloth tunic of a Franciscan friar. As always, Francis needed to step carefully around potential charges of heresy in an age when the Church severely punished renegades. Moreover, he could not allow Clare to wander the countryside with him or the other friars, or to camp overnight with them. But he arranged for Clare and her women companions to live in one of the chapels he had rebuilt, where they could devote themselves to a sacred life of prayer and poverty, exactly as he did.

As we have seen, too, Dōgen pioneered new opportunities for women seeking to devote themselves fully to spiritual life. Orthodox Japanese Buddhism refused to admit women on equal footing with men. Dōgen welcomed them. Several women, including Ryōnen and Eshin and Egi, lived and practiced as monastics in Dōgen's secluded monastery in the mountains of Echizen. In the *Shōbōgenzō* Dōgen stated emphatically that both men and women can realize the Way.

Rūmī also taught female disciples, some of whom became accomplished Sufi masters themselves; in doing so they followed in the tradition of the eighth-century female Sufi saint Rābi'a al-'Adawiyya and other precursors. Rūmī, as we have observed, wrote of Sufi spiritual ideas using standard gender symbolism, describing intellect as male and ego as female; in actual practice, therefore, a woman of purified intellect and spiritual aspiration might be designated "male" and a man enslaved to ego might be "female." Ideally, the intellect and ego, male and female, should abide in harmony.

However, Rūmī used this kind of terminology in ways that sound disconcertingly sexist today, and in ways impossible to find in writings of Francis or Dōgen. They do not declare, as Rūmī does, that "your ego is indeed a woman—it is worse than a woman, for the woman is a part of evil, your ego the whole." Rūmī also makes assertions such as "Women are for children and satisfying passion."[1]

Given Rūmī's fluid use of the terms "man" and "woman," a reader might find it tantalizing at first glance to conclude that he destabilizes what philosopher Michel Foucault calls the artificial binary of constructed and regulated heterosexual gender categories, and that in assigning "male" spiritual qualities to some women, and "female" spiritual qualities to some men, Rūmī "queers" the conventional distinctions—to use our contemporary terminology—and moves freely within a symbolic discourse of non-essentialist multiplicity in ways that might be approved by readers of such diverse feminist scholars as, for example, Judith Butler, Monique Wittig, Luce Irigaray, or Julia Kristeva. On closer inspection, however, it may be argued that Rūmī's technique does not destabilize gender categories in a way that feminist scholars would advocate, but instead reinforces those categories within a powerfully determined linguistic and social system of patriarchy. Moreover, there is the obvious fact that the spiritual nomenclature Rūmī inherited still generally assigns superior status to "masculine" attributes over "feminine" ones; whether the individual who personifies those attributes is actually perceived, via social constructs, as "male" or "female," this fact remains.

While it may seem unfair to judge a thirteenth-century spiritual teacher and writer by twenty-first century standards, the truth is that Dōgen consistently holds up to such scrutiny when we look at his attitudes toward women. It is a pity that Rūmī does not. This is perhaps the greatest puzzlement Rūmī holds for a modern reader. Nevertheless, in other contexts he also wrote admiringly of women and he honored those in his own life, including female Sufis whom he fully respected as equals, and those women honored him as well. In considering Rūmī's impressive but imperfect legacy, this is crucial to acknowledge.

Of course, Francis, Dōgen, and Rūmī could not know that three-quarters of a millennium after their lifetimes we would appraise efforts they made to welcome women into religious life. They offer us historical models that we can cite today, with relative degrees of enthusiasm or caution, as we continue to push within our own spiritual traditions for women's full equality.

Francis, Dōgen, and Rūmī also feel modern and relevant to our lives because they offer examples of an embodied spirituality, instructing us that our human bodies can serve sacred purposes. In our postmodern secular materialist culture, most people fail to recognize that the body can provide locus for spiritual awakening. In fact, however, body and spiritual practices can link together, intimately. They can support one another.

As discussed in Chapter Two, Francis arrived at this understanding belatedly. The body, to him, served as a battleground. Like other Christians in the Middle Ages he struggled to subdue the flesh in what he considered its interminable war against the spirit, and, as we have seen, he punished his body until it broke. He treated it like a beast of burden. He called it "Brother Donkey" as it weakened and sickened, festering with sores. Francis, who as a young man had indulged his physical appetites through riotous carousing, died scrawny and blind and feverish and crusted with oozing wounds. Near the end, however, he realized his error and asked forgiveness of his body. Francis provides a cautionary tale. If you divorce flesh from spiritual practice, you may fight the body to make it submit, as Francis did in the Middle Ages, or you may shape the body as an object, as many do today by using cosmetic surgeries, hoping to make the body conform to standards decreed by a relentless multi-million-dollar advertising industry. Either way, you make the mistake of materialism, thinking that the body is merely a carnal package inside of which your "self" exists.

Dōgen averted this mistake, as we have noted. Like other Zen Buddhists, he never posited a dualistic war between the flesh and spiritual life. All Buddhists know, moreover, that the Buddha himself counseled a "middle way" in regard to both asceticism and hedonism, advising moderation. In Zen Buddhist practice, as Dōgen reminds us, the body serves as the vehicle for enlightenment. *Zazen* meditation is grounded in the body, in its seated yogic posture, in its walking and working, in its breathing. "The Way is surely attained with the body," Dōgen avers.[2] He also speaks not simply of the body, but of the integrated "body-mind," and, like all Buddhists, he describes a body-mind that simultaneously functions as a differentiated entity and is empty of fixed, permanent substance.

Dōgen's description of the interconnected body-mind has profound implications for Western understanding. Currently in academic circles, scholars influenced by Lacan's neo-Freudianism and by Foucault often discourse on "the body" as a socially constructed subject and a contested site of institutional power, and so on, while they implicitly maintain the West's traditional Cartesian mind-body dichotomy. Dōgen rejects that dichotomy. It is interesting to note, however, that researchers at the vanguard of contemporary Western medicine have begun to reject it as well, discovering evidence for an intimately connected body-mind. Contemporary brain research, as well, shows evidence of a strongly interdependent body-mind entity.

Rūmī thought of the body in dualistic terms of the material and spiritual—of which the latter, he said, comprises two of the three levels of existence, the third being Allah—but within this dichotomy Rūmī praised with his customary enthusiasm the material body *and* the spirit. The body, formed in the image of Allah, in fact serves as the outward manifestation of spirit. When spirit frees itself of ego and ascends toward the heavenly liberation of *fanā'* and of *baqā'*, then both body and spirit can reflect the grace of God. Rūmī's praise of the body becomes lavish when he writes in erotic metaphors of the longing for the Divine Beloved. And his claim that the body may serve as a vehicle for the purest bliss of the spirit becomes tangible when Sufi dervishes spin beatifically for hours, as Rūmī did himself in the streets of Konya.

Many people today yearn to reintegrate body and spirit in sacred practice. The seated meditation known to Dōgen, the ecstatic dance known to Rūmī—or practices of yoga, or tai chi, or qigong, or sexual Tantra, or other body-oriented spiritual practices, including simply walking attentively in the woods or in a park—bring us physically into the numinous with vigor and keenness of presence. Dōgen and Rūmī, especially, can serve as models for affirming the power of the body in experiencing the sacred.

Francis, Dōgen, and Rūmī also feel modern, and continue to matter, because they show us ways to free ourselves of attitudes that contribute directly to our current environmental emergencies. This bears repeating at length:

In regard to the natural world, and the relation of humans to land, water, sky, and living creatures, Francis achieved something revolutionary in Western culture. Unlike his European contemporaries, who believed that the Biblical book of Genesis authorized "mankind" to rule in lordly dominion over lesser animals and the vast realms of Creation, Francis of Assisi viewed nature as the garden of God's handiwork, all of it sacred, and he considered humans but one member in a glorious kinship of Brother Sun and Sister Pine and Brother Wolf and Sister Rain. Francis shows us a path the West could have taken centuries ago.

Instead, because the standard notion of "man's" dominance over nature has prevailed, we now face calamity. The world beloved by Francis sizzles with heat trapped by greenhouse gases, with killer storms and droughts, while the Earth's glaciers and polar ice caps melt away. If we take the view of Francis, when we pump gigatons of carbon dioxide and methane gases into the atmosphere, foul the oceans with plastic garbage, burn down the rainforests of the Amazon and Indonesia, eliminate bird and butterfly habitat to construct acres of McMansions, poison our soil and water with pesticides, and generate massive radioactive nuclear waste, it not only means that humans are committing collective suicide—by taking other creatures with us into oblivion and devastating the planet we murder God's Creation. It is sacrilege. Consider the plants and animals, the insects and fish and birds hailed as "brother" and "sister" by Francis; each month humans snuff out entire species, erasing them forever from planet Earth. Meanwhile humans cram other "sister" and "brother" animals into factory farms, cage them, bloat them with drugs and artificial hormones, then slaughter them. If we eat them, if we take their once-living bodies into our own as nourishment, how many of us do so with reverence, as the native peoples of America did, professing thanks to these animals for the gift of their lives? Very few. Most people gobble these "brother" and "sister" creatures as junk food, served up with fries and a Coke. Francis calls us, in the twenty-first century, to bear witness to these horrors. Whether we call ourselves liberals or conservatives makes no difference. Francis teaches us another way to live on this planet: a sacred way.

Dōgen's mystical approach to nature was consistent with his Zen practice. As we have seen, he expressed a profound fondness for blossoming plum and fireflies and the autumn moon, but not in accord with a typically Japanese form of aestheticism, and not as a sentimentalist or a nature Romantic, and not as a pan-spiritualist. Rather, Dōgen's experience of the sacred in nature was shaped by Zen's avowal that the Absolute and the Relative aspects of reality are identical.

Writing from the non-dual view of the Absolute, of Oneness, Dōgen refused to discriminate between insentient and sentient creatures, claiming that all elements of the natural world realize universal, original Buddha-nature; writing as well from the view of the Relative, of differentiation, he claimed that all beings speak the Dharma in their individual voices. When seen truly, nature is experienced in its wholeness: in the Absolute view, mountains and rivers are empty of inherent substance, within a great, interdependent cosmic matrix of

Oneness; simultaneously, in the Relative view, mountains and rivers and indeed all beings fully manifest their own specificity, their unique "thusness," emerging in their vivid being-in-the-moment into a profuse natural world of distinctive phenomena and within the flux of arising and passing away.

This may seem esoteric, but it has immediate and straightforward implications in our age of environmental crisis. Dōgen prompts us to realize that a maple tree, for example, exists not as a decoration on a lawn, not as a piece of lumber. In its total exertion of universal Buddha-nature in the particularity of itself, in its singular thusness, it has intrinsic value *as itself,* simply by being a maple tree. A unique sentient being, the maple thrives as a breathing creature, one that inhales carbon dioxide, exhales oxygen. At the same time, as a fellow inhabitant of our communal earth, its roots and leaves inseparable from rain, sun, breezes, and the root systems of its neighboring trees, the maple exists interwoven with us and with universal Buddha-nature, its cells alive with shared intelligence and a secret inner fire. If we utilize it by chopping wood, we must do so with the same respect and thanksgiving that we bring to our liturgies in the zendo or church, the temple or mosque. Dōgen also helps us to see that a mountain is not a thing in the landscape placed there expediently for blasting and bulldozing and drilling, so that people might empty it of coal and ore. A mountain "walks." Dōgen said this, in part, as a way of pointing to the impermanence of something that seems solid and enduring, but we can extend his statement to say that a mountain walks in the vast scope of tectonic forces and geologic time, moving too slowly for human perception but moving and changing nonetheless. A mountain breathes, through its plants and trees. A mountain has live veins of running water. A mountain, too, is a unique sentient being that also exists within our mutual world community. Indigenous peoples of the Americas, of Australia and Europe, of Africa and Asia, the so-called "primitive" cultures, always have known this.

Rūmī, a city dweller who differed from Francis and Dōgen by not feeling a need to retreat into the wilderness of the high peaks, nevertheless shows acute sensitivity to nature. Rūmī, like all Sufis, saw every creature as a living embodiment of Allah's Creation, and viewed that earthly Creation, in turn, as a beauteous veil concealing the radiant face of God. Rūmī wrote of the sea, of gazelles and jasmine and nightingales, in exuberant celebration. He wrote of the sun, symbol of Divine Majesty, and water, symbol of purifying Grace. The earthly gardens he adored, sumptuous with roses, hinted at the heavenly garden of the supreme Beloved. Rūmī reminds us of the sacrality of nature.

Equally important, this trio of enlightened teachers remains meaningful because they show us how to practice and express spiritual love. Francis, as noted earlier, radically modified ideals of courtly love by casting them in sacred terminology. As God's chivalric knight he devoted himself to his Lady Poverty. In doing so he achieved not only a poverty of material goods but a poverty of ego, and he demonstrated that a wandering beggar of medieval Italy could emulate the selfless life of Jesus, showing generous and authentic love to all, even those most scorned by society. Many people today will balk at choosing a life of severe poverty. Yet Francis shows us that by drastically simplifying our existence to focus on what truly matters, we free ourselves to better express compassion for people in need. Looking at Francis and his embrace of lepers, you can ask, "Who are the 'lepers' in my own midst? Are they homeless people? Are they immigrant families and refugees? Are they people addicted to opioids? How might I learn to serve them? What can I let go of, what can I relinquish in my cluttered modern life, so that I might live more simply and in loving service to others?"

Dōgen, by contrast, did not seek out the hurt and the rejected, but manifested loving compassion by welcoming through the open doors of his monastery all men and women, regardless of social class, who found their way there, those who ached in spirit and sincerely thirsted for dharma teaching. He demonstrated love by guiding them toward the healing of enlightenment, a process in which compassion for others arises naturally. In his instructions for a proper life Dōgen emphasized civility, gentleness of speech, and "kind mind" (although admittedly in his writings he could be curt at times in criticizing other Buddhist sects and schools). Today, in our own polarized and often brutish society, with its vitriolic Internet postings, its road rage, its screaming tirades on radio talk shows and TV, Dōgen's model of loving compassion seems tonic. Looking at Dōgen each of us can ask, "How can I live more beneficently? Amid all my struggles, how can I make my own life resemble a 'Temple of Eternal Peace,' and who can I welcome there?"

Rūmī offered yet another interpretation of spiritual love: as a whirling, perfervid erotic longing for the Divine Beloved, a desire for the drunken bliss of selfless disintegration into God and the subsequent abiding in His universal Essence. As a Sufi saint he believed that love pulses throughout the cosmos, emanating from Allah. Rūmī's ecstatic love for the Divine found earthly focus in his enraptured and passionate spiritual friendship with Shams-i-Tabrīzī. The erotic fed his spiritual life. Rūmī teaches us that Eros can be more than a means for selling lip gloss and designer jeans in fashion magazines. Eros can speak aloud the mystical name of the Divine. Looking at Rūmī, each of us can ask, "How can I invest my passionate sensuality with spirit? How can I imbue spirit with the vigorous life-energy of the erotic?"

Francis, Dōgen, and Rūmī also matter to us today in showing the importance of balancing vigorous life in community with periodic retreat into silence and seclusion for spiritual renewal. Their example reminds us that we need to take the backward step into prayer and meditation. This is not escapism; we still need friends and family; we also must continue to work with the messiness of everyday living, which can be a great teacher; moreover, we must attend to the pressing emergencies of a chaotic world. Yet we also need relief from its incessant clamor. Today, when so many people feel overwhelmed and frazzled, when their lives feel superficial, frantic, and hollow at the core, Francis and Dōgen and Rūmī show us the central importance of frequent withdrawal, so that we can reconnect deeply with the sacred.

For many seekers of spiritual fulfillment in the twenty-first century, nagging questions arise regarding how to achieve the necessary balance, and how to resolve conflicts between living in the spirit and living in a voraciously materialistic society. For our trio of Christian, Buddhist, and Muslim teachers in the thirteenth century, similar questions led each to devise a unique and bold solution.

Admittedly, Francis's is one that few will wish to emulate. As an ideal of selflessness and service, however, it continues to inspire. As we have seen, Francis often retreated from the secular world, finding solitude to fast and pray. He also practiced within a Christian Church that boasted a nine-hundred-year-old tradition of monastic community—and he rejected it. European monasteries of the 1200s had become staid and lethargic, or, at the opposite extreme, had become luxurious hideaways for wealthy nobles who wished to dine well and pray at their leisure and thereby guarantee a future place for their souls in heaven. Francis refused to set foot in those places. He wished to roam the countryside and work with the poor and with those who suffer, as Jesus had.

Like so much accomplished by Francis, these modest acts proved revolutionary. Throngs of eager young men joined Francis, emulating his vow of ragged poverty, merrily tramping through fields and villages to spread a simple message of Christian love. Francis and his legions of friars established a wandering community. Eager women also flocked to Francis's chapel to establish a spiritual community of their own.

Eventually, however, the friars wanted comforts of a monastery. They wanted the security of official rules and doctrines. When this happened, Francis resigned as head of the Franciscan Order. He continued his errant ways. His most loyal followers remained with him, balancing retreat with communal life. Though few people today will wish to adopt the drastic choices Francis made, he still can offer us a stirring example: in constantly negotiating ways to include both solitary spiritual practice and community in his life, Francis shows us the value of listening to the wisdom of our authentic inner voice, no matter where it leads.

Dōgen's solution can inspire spiritually motivated people who yearn to create radical social alternatives by dropping out of the mainstream. Dōgen shunned the lavish Buddhist monasteries of Japan as uncompromisingly as Francis spurned those of Christian Europe, but Dōgen chose a different remedy. In the wild, distant mountains of coastal Japan, far from the worldly affairs of Kyoto, he built his ideal monastery. Here, in the "Temple of Eternal Peace," he could train Zen monks the way he believed they should be trained, in the rigorously authentic style of Buddhism that he first experienced in China. Dōgen's monastery of Eihei-ji functioned as a radical experiment, a place of withdrawal from society that also offered a utopian model for it. Dōgen believed that when conducted properly, monasticism could show a person how to actively live Zen's ethical precepts, how to practice solo meditation, and also how to live with others of like mind in harmonious community. Today, in America and elsewhere, Buddhist monastic centers serve as homes for small groups of ordained men and women, while attracting larger numbers of people for retreats and weekend teachings, people with jobs and families who seek the tranquil atmosphere, the inspiration, and the spiritual support that monasteries offer. These people benefit from what Dōgen envisioned and created.

Rūmī's solution regarding the balance between solitary spiritual practice and community life remains the most compelling for many spiritual seekers today. Islam has no monastic tradition, so Rūmī, deciding whether to live in the world or to seek withdrawal, compromised. In Konya he maintained a vivacious family life as a husband and father, worked industriously as a legal scholar and preacher, strolled the market plaza, and regaled friends with nights of dancing and music. He interspersed these with periods of *khalwa*, of seclusion, in which he prayed and fasted. Rūmī, as the saying goes, was *in* the world, but not *of* it. For a twenty-first century person not affiliated with a church, a Buddhist center, a mosque, a temple, or other religious group yet trying to maintain an authentic life of prayer or meditation while enjoying a career, a gregarious social circle, and a romantic relationship or a marriage and parenthood, Rūmī offers an appealing reminder that such a life is possible.

We also should remember that spiritual retreat is not always effortless and blissful; in fact, as the personal examples of Francis, Dōgen, and Rūmī remind us, retreat can be arduous, a process of self-sacrifice, of ego-surrender, that often includes struggle and turmoil. Hidden traumas and challenging emotions can arise. Powerful temptations to quit can feel irresistibly enticing. These three spiritual teachers can serve us today as models of perseverance, showing us how to ride the turbulence and stay with it until it subsides. As we sit in retreat we can silently invoke them; we can invite Francis or Dōgen or Rūmī—and other spiritual mentors and guides who speak to us from across centuries and geographical distances and religious traditions—to be with us, to help steady us, to help us access our own inner strength as we discover equanimity and clarity.

As we have seen in Chapter Three, the Christian saint from Assisi, the Sōtō Zen Buddhist, and the Muslim Sufi matter today because they give us poems that not only delight but that retain power to beam relevant spiritual information across seventy-five decades.

Of Francis's original corpus of verses, "The Canticle of Brother Sun" remains one of the very few still extant, and evokes admiration not only for its gentle lyricism and its sweet laudations but for its inclusive vision. That vision encompasses all animate things, all the living manifestations of earth, fire, water and air, and sees them as members of an abundant, generous cosmic family that reveals to humans the bounty and blessings of God. It speaks powerfully to us today.

Poems of Rūmī and Dōgen also continue to speak to us—of desolation and contentment, the uses of language and of silence, and of life's transience. As we have observed, in Rūmī's work, the aching separation from his revered friend, Shams, also symbolizes the estrangement of the soul from God. In the work of Dōgen, wistful poems of longing for home can symbolize, as well, a yearning for the experience known in Zen as "true home," or enlightened Buddhanature. A second theme common to the poetry of Rūmī and Dōgen is that of language and silence. Though Rūmī's immense outpouring of more than 35,000 poems in the *Rubaiyat*, the *Dīwān-e Shams-e Tabrīzī* and the *Mathnawī* constitute a remarkable gushing and surging of language, Rūmī also professes to value silence, when prolixity threatens to blunt his raw contact with reality, or when he encounters the ineffable. Dōgen, too, works adroitly in the interstices between language and silence. He crafts words sparingly and precisely. He uses them, as Zen poetry often does, to simultaneously delineate objects in the natural world and to hint at experiences literally beyond description. Ephemerality, a third poetic theme shared by Rūmī and Dōgen, finds disparate expression in each writer; Rūmī conveys the flux of outer and inner worlds through sprawling panoramas of ever-shifting, phantasmagoric "cinematic" imagery, while Dōgen describes impermanence in small, exactly focused "snapshots": dewdrops on a blade of grass.

We have noted, too, that the Sufi poet and the Zen poet utilize the image of the self as an unmoored boat. Rūmī employs the image to suggest the self battered at sea, struggling toward God, till destroyed by the smashing waves and thus released into an exultant new awareness of liberation, or *fanā'*. Dōgen's use of the image, by contrast, suggests a different state of enlightenment, one characterized by imperturbable serenity. The boat image is not the only one shared by Rūmī and Dōgen; they frequently use moon imagery as well. The lunar images gain special power when the two poets use them to symbolize spiritual illumination.

The ultimate spiritual illumination, of course, results from neutralizing the "me," the petty self. Francis, Dōgen, and Rūmī agree on this, and it forms the vital core of their mystical understanding. Francis wrote that spiritual virtues emanate from God, and that no one can possess them who "does not die to self." This dying to self—eradicating the narcissistic disease of ego obsession—corresponds to the Zen *satori* and the Sufi *fanā'*.

We in the twenty-first century still learn much from these medieval poems.

* * *

Equally crucial, Francis, Dōgen, and Rūmī matter today because they serve us as wisdom sources. This wisdom derives from their mystical experiences. Francis and Dōgen and Rūmī exemplify the life of the mystic's path—life devoted to direct, selfless experience of the sacred in each moment.

Mysticism is a "process," according to Bernard McGinn in his monumental study *The Presence of God: A History of Western Christian Mysticism*. It is not merely the consummate experience of unifying mundane life with the Divine, but every movement leading to that experience and everything that flows from it afterward. This process of mysticism, he says, is "a way of life."[3] Philip Sheldrake, in *Spaces for the Sacred: Place, Memory and Identity*, refers to McGinn's work and agrees with him that "mysticism, if we continue to use the word, is essentially a process or way of life rather than a set of isolated experiences."[4]

Thomas Merton, too, antedating McGinn and Sheldrake, speaks of the process of mysticism as a way of life, citing in his essay "The English Mystics" the anonymous fourteenth-century author of the *Cloud of Unknowing*. Merton calls the neutralization of ego "a dying to the individual essence" and writes that this mystical way of life is "a rare grace...rare by its very simplicity.... It is a way of life...in which one must learn to act by not acting and know by not knowing: to have one desire alone which is not really a desire but a kind of desirelessness, an openness, a habitual freedom in the sense of self-abandonment."[5]

(We may compare this with Pierre Hadot's contention that philosophy should be a way of life: not theoretical, but a dynamic process, a vital and transformative practice of living, best exemplified by Platonists, Stoics, and Epicureans of the ancient Greek, Hellenistic, and Roman worlds but still available to us today. Moreover, according to Hadot, this way of life called philosophy, this daily quest for wisdom, is a way of utilizing reason to attain cosmic consciousness, and of acting in service to justice as a means of benefiting the human community. Thus it might supplement the mystical approach.)[6]

Francis, Dōgen, and Rūmī show us the mystical way of life in abundance.

While any person can open to natural, mystical experiences, some cultivate this openness assiduously and train to perfect it. When people develop natural physical abilities we call them athletes; when they develop natural creative abilities we call them artists; when they develop their natural connection to the sacred that we all share, and maintain it as a way of life, we call them mystics.

As they develop their ability to sustain mystical experience, it places them in a relationship to society that is inherently antinomian.

Though often appropriated by religious institutions after their deaths, their charismatic example diluted and their teachings neutralized, those who are mystics tend during their lifetimes to exist as outsiders. We have seen this with Francis, Dōgen, and Rūmī, and it remains true today: in standard social realms dominated both by the hollow blandishments of *secular materialism* and the stifling religious platitudes of the *holy* the mystic travels between the two, living instead in the realm of the *sacred*. In the discussion that follows, reference to the "holy," the "secular," and the "sacred" modify the well-known terminology of "sacred" and "profane" pioneered by Mircea Eliade in his classic text *The Sacred and the Profane: The Nature of Religion:*[7]

What is the *sacred*? Vibrant, feral, potent, the sacred is life-enhancing and, because it can unleash stupendous energies, perilous. Experience of the sacred is penetratingly heartfelt, soulfully connected and awake, imbued with spiritual force. It is the realm of enigma and wonder, of charged and often eccentric beauty. It links incomprehensible vastness of eternity to the immediate right-here, right-now. Often we experience the sacred manifesting in nature, in creative work, and in artful human habitations that harmonize with nature's designs. We experience it in communing with others, with our deepest selves, and with the cosmos when those selves lapse into subsidence while opening into a brilliance of pure awareness.

(This definition of the sacred may be compared with that of Paul Ricoeur, in *Figuring the Sacred: Religion, Narrative, and Imagination,* who elaborates on Eliade in organizing his own "phenomenology of the sacred" around five specific traits: the sacred is awesome and powerful; the sacred is a hierophany, the numinous revealing itself in space and time, both verbally and non-verbally; the sacred reveals itself not only in signs to be contemplated but through behaviors that require actions performed in mythic ritual; the sacred is dramatically expressed in nature "in symbolically saying itself"; the sacred universe displays a logic of meaning rooted in symbolic correspondences between celestial and earthly, eternal and mundane.)[8]

What is the realm of *secular materialism*? It characterizes a world bereft of spirit, one that values only the material realm and belittles sacred experience: the world of money-grubbing and heartless commerce instead of sharing; of brutal competition instead of kindness; of tedious, pointless jobs instead of life-fulfilling vocations; of bloodlust and warfare instead of temperance and peace; of strip malls instead of garden cities, and strip mines instead of wilderness; of cheapness and efficiency instead of refinement and beauty; of porn instead of Eros; of tawdry mass-market spectacles and vapid entertainments instead of art; of novelty instead of progress; of crude scientific reductionism, narrowly obsessed with measuring and quantifying, with data, drives, and "dead matter," instead of a noble, expansive science that employs technological tools and the majestic language of advanced mathematics to probe the sublimities of the cosmos, and to open-mindedly investigate the full range of natural possibilities, including those deemed "supernatural" or spiritual. Secular materialism breeds what Thoreau called "lives of quiet desperation." (Incidentally, it can manifest as capitalism or as communism. The main difference between the two systems lies in who controls the means of material production and how the material profits get distributed.) The man or woman devoted to mystical life moves unimpeded through the secular materialist world, as Francis or Dōgen or Rūmī did, perceiving it clearly but without attachment. That spiritless world holds no allure.

What is the *holy*? Equally spiritless, it is that narrow range of the sacred brought under control and ostensibly "consecrated" through religious authority. In fact, the holy represents the sacred after it has been desacralized, when it is routinized, tamed, and regulated, deprived of its profoundly enigmatic quality and its numinous force and enshrined in official institutions. The holy is a drab, perfunctory religiosity of formulaic ritual, of rote observances and hollow faith. The holy often manifests in theocracies, in many churches and temples, in state-sanctioned piety and priestly dogma. If tainted by the rigid certainties of fundamentalist ideology, the holy can lose its tepid blandness to veer into religious fanaticism. If the zealotry becomes acute, and further poisoned by socio-political imperatives, perceived victimhood, and a rage for vengeance, it can launch holy war, crusades, and terrorism. Francis, Dōgen, and Rūmī moved beyond the holy.

What are some of the universal commonalities in mystical experience? What do Francis, Dōgen, and Rūmī help us to understand about the mystical path?

William James, in his classic *The Varieties of Religious Experience*, lists four primary qualities of the mystical experience: it is ineffable; it has a noetic quality; it is transient; it is passive. (The ineffability and passivity of mystical experience will be challenged in our discussion that follows.)

Evelyn Underhill, in *Mysticism*, responds to James' delineation of mystical qualities by listing four of her own. She states the characteristics of the mystical path as follows: "true mysticism is active and practical, not passive and theoretical"; "its aims are wholly transcendental and spiritual"; the "changeless One" which the mystic seeks is "not merely the Reality of all that is, but also a living and personal Object of Love"; and "living union with this One…is a definite state or form of enhanced life."[9]

As we did in expanding Eliade's and Ricoeur's definitions of "sacred," however, we also may adapt and modify James's and Underhill's characterizations of mysticism:

First, we can say that mysticism is *unique in constituting a selfless experience of Ultimate Reality.* Because it perceives the Absolute—the Infinite, the Divine, Godhead, the cosmos, the Eternal—directly, freed of the narrow filter of "I-me-mine," the mystical way of experience is distinctive in that it occurs outside of established theological frameworks based in doctrine or priestly authority or, in our own era, outside of findings based on scientific research. (Although it occurs outside of scientific modes of understanding, mystical experience need not contradict them, however. It also may confirm them.

Mystical ways of knowing in the thirteenth century could supplement the empirical-inductive approach of the new Western science, pioneered by Roger Bacon; in regard to scientific research today, the twenty-first century mystic who intuits that our material world lacks inherent substance or permanence and exists as pulsing energy will find herself agreeing with contemporary physicists.)

What we are calling mysticism's *selfless experience of Ultimate Reality* is a direct engagement with the sacred; James would describe this as a way of knowing, but not of analytical knowing; rather the "noetic quality" of an experience of mystical awakening exists as a state of "insight into depths of truth unplumbed by the discursive intellect." Such states, he writes, "are illuminations, revelations." [10] During the thirteenth century of Francis, Dōgen, and Rūmī the "states of insight" and the "illuminations" and "revelations" of mystics offered contrast to the rational ways of knowing promoted by the era's philosophers, including Ibn Rushd (also known as Averroes) of Islamic Spain, whose work was translated into Latin in the early 1200s, or Thomas Aquinas, who died in 1274, a year after the death of Rūmī. If we look farther back historically, the "states of insight" experienced by mystics such as Francis, Dōgen, and Rūmī may be contrasted, as well, with those of the ancient Stoics. Seneca and Marcus Aurelius extolled a life of sober joyousness, virtue, equanimity, and wisdom that transcends the self to experience the cosmic Whole, which Seneca called *toti se inserens mundo*, or "plunging oneself into the totality of the world"[11]—an aim similar to mystical practice—but the Stoics employed spiritual exercises and reason to accomplish this. The mystic, on the other hand, may employ reason in its proper sphere (Dōgen's reasoning in philosophical treatises of the *Shōbōgenzō* is rigorous), but will forego it as a primary method in favor of *selfless experience of Ultimate Reality,* going directly to the Source.

Second, we can say that mystical experience is accompanied by a *radical transforming of personal consciousness, opening it toward Oneness and Love.* Whether ephemeral or more enduring, the experience is marked by a sense of the vast, majestic scope and astonishing perfection of the universe, of profound interconnectedness, and corresponding feelings of awe, thanksgiving, modesty, and wellbeing. To become open to naturally occurring mystical experience by dropping our habits of oblivious distraction requires persistence and vigor, requires a seeker driven—literally beyond reason—to directly experience its luminosity. After such arduous spiritual preparation, mystical experience may arrive seemingly unbidden. Yet, as James observes, this resolute activity of the mystic also requires an element of surrender. In moments of awakened consciousness the mystic feels as if his or her "own will were in abeyance."[12] When willful demands of ego have paused, and feelings of separation from others melt away, a spontaneous sense of all-pervading at-Oneness with the universe and an upwelling of loving kindness and solicitude flows without impediment. Perhaps merely for the brief duration of the mystical experience itself, perhaps with reverberations that persist for much longer—depending on the depth of the experience, and on the ability to incorporate it and keep it alive—the transformed consciousness is illumined by Love, by the light of the opened heart. Evelyn Underhill, as we have noted above, refers to this as "the changeless One" experienced as "a living and personal Object of Love." We have seen this with Francis and Rūmī and, in modified terms, with Dōgen.

Third, we can say that, as part of the radical transformation of consciousness, mystical events *alter the experience of space-time.* Because periods of mystical encounter allow a man or woman to directly perceive the "changeless One" in its trans-temporal reality, the subjective sense of linear time characteristic of the relative world of phenomena may shift, may leap "backward" or "forward," may seem to accelerate or slow down or stop altogether. Regardless of how time may be perceived subjectively during mystical experiences, however, viewed objectively or "by the clock" they are generally short, occurring in flashes of only seconds or minutes. James notes that experiences of mystical awakening are marked by their transience: "They cannot be sustained for long," he writes, but they can be remembered and their "inner richness and importance" lingers.[13] However, such discrete, ephemeral events can occur in sequences over a period of hours or days. The longer a person sustains a series of mystical experiences, and the more frequently such flares of illumination occur, the more potent and life-changing they become. These experiences are also "ineffable," according to James[14]—but here he opens himself to controversy. For while the mystical experience may be indescribable in all of its sublime details, Francis to some degree and Dōgen and Rūmī to a much greater extent succeeded through poetry in evoking at least the atmosphere of such charged experiences. Dōgen also used prose to convey the tenor of mystical awareness through his radically innovative use of language in the *Shōbōgenzō*, which allowed him to make stunning, instantaneous leaps from the Relative world of phenomena to the formless Absolute and back again in the flicker of a few sentences.

Fourth, we can say that a person may sense mystical experience as one of two distinct *movements* of consciousness, culminating in *stillness*. It may be felt as expansiveness, a heightened sense of lucidity and spaciousness, or as contraction, into an enclosed, alert state of deep, narrowed focus and tranquility. These two movements of outward or inward may occur within the same experience or exclusively of each other. As the distinction between outer and inner dissolves, the experience becomes one of pure Being in non-action.

Francis, Dōgen, and Rūmī displayed all of these characteristics of mysticism. They arrived at distinctive means of experiencing Ultimate Reality. They underwent personal transformations, marked by love and compassion. Following visionary or other extreme psychic states they described altered consciousness of space-time in selfless experiences of direct encounter with the Absolute, and in the motion toward stillness of an awakened mind.

Throughout, they maintained an unorthodox way of abiding in the world that moved deftly between both secular materialism and the holy to actively experience the sacred. As mystics they realized that everything is alive and that all life is, in truth, a celebratory miracle within the grandeur of a flawless universe. They realized this in exceptional abundance.

Skeptics may complain that this sounds too airy-fairy, too trite, too serene. Mystical experience, they scoff, is seldom nice. Indeed, such an experience can blast a person's psyche into reeling terror and confusion: it is a fearsome thing to fall into the hands of the living God. Some will remind us that the word "panic" derives from the Greek *panikos*, "of Pan," to describe the emotion of glimpsing the horned, goat-footed god; who would desire that sort of mystical encounter? What about Thracian priestesses of Bacchus tearing the flesh of animals in their wine-soaked, frenzied nightlong dances in the hills? What about a prophet of Israel flung to his knees, shielding his eyes from Jehovah's awful radiance? What about cowering shepherds, "sore afraid" at the startling vision of an Angel? Or a medieval nun who locks herself in a cell for years, to swoon as a bride of Christ in ranting prayer and blissful hysteria? What about a Hindu holy man of Nepal, shaken and crazed by the blood-hunger of the goddess Durga? Or a shaman wracked by convulsions as a god seizes his body from inside and begins to howl? What about a ragged man pacing in the subway, eyes glittering as he shouts, "I am the Messiah!" Wild hallucinations, voices, derangement, insanity, all of it unnerving: here, its critics allege, lurks "mysticism" in its monstrous glory.

We may answer that mystical encounter with the sacred occurs in people who display many different stages of spiritual growth. For those who have begun to open into mystical experience but retain an adamant sense of personal self, the ego may inflate in grandiose spiritual delusions. Or, if anxious and uncertain, it may stiffen against what it fears as a threat of dissolution, prompting ferocious internal combat between the resisting self and a person's deeper and equally desperate yearning for transcendence. The greater the ego-strength, the greater the struggle. Under these circumstances it may seem, indeed, a fearsome thing to fall into God's hands.

For those who try to force the mystical experience and hasten it through intense religious rituals or intoxicating drugs without proper teaching and guidance, a vast, abrupt bursting open into sacred experience may quickly expand the consciousness. It comes as too much, too soon. It feels like plugging a light bulb not into a wall sconce, but directly into the vast power grid itself. Subjected to such enormous voltage the unprepared ego feels tiny, vulnerable, very fragile, and precariously exposed. Instead of encountering the sacred in a brilliantly liberating psychic breakthrough, a person experiences psychic breakdown. The delicate ego shatters. The person experiences not mysticism, but a surge of madness.

Francis once saw a six-winged angel. Dōgen threw off "body and mind." Rūmī spun in ecstatic connection with the Beloved. These were extreme experiences. They were transformative. Yet Francis, Dōgen, and Rūmī did not evince madness; they displayed a luminous sanity. They did so because, over time, each had surrendered himself in a way that diminished the hugely selfish, obscuring "I" sufficiently to live in direct contact with numinous reality. The vestigial "I" that remained in each of these three spiritual teachers was not fragile or brittle. It was flexible and adaptable, able to thrive in the daily world, able to remain open, permeable, and to receive continuous nourishment from the sacred. Here we see exemplary models of natural mysticism.

One further issue remains. In theistic traditions, mystics often suffer the impossibility of achieving final union with God in this life. The solitary seeker experiences years of fruitless searching and longing, feeling bereft or listlessly vacant, adrift in despair, beseeching the Deity while praying ardently and waiting for God's sudden contact. Then it comes: a flash from nowhere. God disorients and spins the person around, knocks the seeker flat, and vanishes, leaving the person breathless with commingled fear and awe. Years of watchful yearning and prayer resume, until God's next thunderous visitation—if it ever comes. This version of mystical life consists of long stagnant periods of spiritual despondency and desire, punctuated by explosions of the sacred then return to dull, searching existence, until final liberation into death and, at last, ultimate union with God in Heaven or in the Eternal.

Francis and Rūmī (because he does not belong to a theistic tradition, we set Dōgen aside for the moment) did not experience God this way. Their mysticism was one of perpetual contact with the divine. Granted, God did appear in rare moments of staggering power, but the Deity also remained, the rest of the time, a blissful presence in the lives of Francis and Rūmī, a divine light always suffusing this broken yet beauteous world.

Proof lies in the return of Francis and Rūmī to this world after their most powerful visionary experiences of God, and their conduct within it. William James writes of the mystical experience in purely psychological terms, describing it as a brief, singular event, in which the lone seeker gains transcendent knowledge. James fails to account for one of the most important aspects of mysticism as Francis and Rūmī experienced it. This is the social dimension, the return to an everyday world of neighbors and villagers in the marketplace, a world now charged with God's presence, with sacred meaning. Francis and Rūmī, though they often withdrew in solitude, also lived robustly in society, the energy of God's presence coursing in their souls; wandering and dancing and singing merrily, proclaiming their closeness to God, they invited everyone to share that energy, to meet God here and now, where the Deity awaits us. The Kingdom of Heaven is at hand.

We may bring Dōgen back to the discussion by noting that, although as a Zen practitioner he made no theistic claims regarding a deity (unlike some Japanese Buddhists of his era—the Pure Land devotees, for example), nevertheless Dōgen, too, invited everyone he met to experience Awakening. After his own deepest experience of such enlightenment while meditating in China, Dōgen returned to his native Japan to share his path with others, feeling continuously the sacred experience, here and now, in every homely activity: strolling with monks, washing his face, sweeping a tatami mat, instructing nuns. Dōgen, unlike Francis and Rūmī, returned to the narrowed society of a monastic world, yet he compassionately invited everyone sincerely devoted to the necessary labor of Awakening to join him within this cloistered society and discover, for themselves, what he had found.

For Francis, Dōgen, and Rūmī, then, mysticism is not a matter of dull, solitary existence interrupted by terrific bursts of the sacred then relapse into anguished and lonely waiting, until death delivers them finally into the Absolute. Mysticism is a process of living vibrantly in the world, amid the ongoing, ever-present manifesting of the sacred, and amid other people, in acts of sharing, joy, and love.

* * *

Perhaps the most compelling reason that Francis, Dōgen, and Rūmī appeal to us now is that they suggest the possibility of inter-religious concord. In the opening decades of the twenty-first century, a "clash of civilizations" and sparring religious ideologies threaten people throughout the world with terrorist assaults and full-scale wars. When we read Francis, Dōgen, and Rūmī we see that a great Christian saint, an illustrious Buddhist teacher, and a renowned Islamic sage, if they had met eight centuries ago, might easily have transcended doctrines unique to their own religions to find agreement in foundational truths of their shared mystical experiences.

Of course, other inspired teachers in Christianity, Buddhism, and Islam could have done the same, in any century. So could accomplished mystical teachers in diverse traditions including Judaism, Hinduism, or Taoism, or Wicca, or the spiritualism of African cultures and the Black Diaspora, or the indigenous shamanic religions throughout the world. Yet, when people on many of these spiritual paths seek inspiring examples of mystical teachers who can support them in their own faith traditions, often they turn to Francis, Dōgen, or Rūmī.

As we have witnessed, these three spiritual leaders shared mutual traits: they grew up in respected families, they traveled widely, they taught students, they founded religious orders, they defied convention, they created enduring literature. Most important, however, the Christian ascetic, the Buddhist teacher, and the Islamic Sufi saint experienced life-altering experiences—direct apprehensions of Ultimate Reality. Each understood these experiences in terms of his own culture and his own religion. Francis, Dōgen, and Rūmī then devised regimens to assist other people in finding ways to set aside the small ego-self and discover a vast, unmediated experience of God, or of Buddha-nature, or of the Divine Beloved. These three are not the same. But each is a particular way of perceiving the Sacred, accessible through what Francis, Dōgen, and Rūmī lived and taught: the mystical path and its opening into love and compassion.

Enlightened contemporaries, Francis and Dōgen and Rūmī, if they could have met, certainly would have recognized in each other qualities of spacious presence, lucidity, laughter, strength, benevolence. They would have spoken to each other, wordlessly, with an eloquent simplicity and an immediacy that would have transcended the limitations of spoken Italian or Japanese or Persian.

In our present Dark Ages of religious wars, of suicide vests and Kalashnikovs, of ethnic cleansing, of massacres and car bombs and drones, of gunfire and beheadings, of *jihad* and evangelical crusade, of resurgent anti-Semitism and white supremacy, of venom in the name of Jesus or Buddha or Allah, these three people—Francis of Assisi, Dōgen Zenji and Jalāl ad-Dīn Rūmī—proffer a vital teaching.

They prove that a Christian and a Buddhist and a Muslim, despite great cultural and theological differences, can join across centuries, showing us a path to the mystical source of all religions: first-hand contact with a numinous reality. Living on such a path, our existence unfolds in moments of sanity and clarity, of fearlessness, of joy amid ineluctable personal suffering, and of openheartedness toward all beings. Such a path—the mystic's journey—can make itself available to each of us. We can find it.

It is here, right now.

Appendix

Some Further Considerations Regarding Mysticism

I contend in the Introduction that "A person who knows mystical experience firsthand...can recognize similar experience described by someone from another era and another culture." Not all scholars agree on this.

We might call my assertion (along with the Saint-Martin quotation, "All mystics speak the same language," which serves as epigraph for the present study) a pronouncement of the Huxleyan perennialist view, after Aldous Huxley's classic, *The Perennial Philosophy*. The dissenting view is known as mystical constructivism, and it argues on epistemological grounds that there is no such thing as a mystical experience of pure consciousness, because all human experiences, including a mystic's claims to realize such consciousness, are mediated by specific cultural beliefs. Thus there cannot exist a uniform template of mystical experience, universally translatable across history and across cultures; rather, we can speak only of a pluralism of diverse mystical events, each constructed and shaped by an individual's unique concepts and experiences, temporal and geographical location, language, and social conditioning.

Perhaps the most forceful advocate of this constructivist view is Steven Katz, author of "Language, Epistemology and Mysticism," included in his *Mysticism and Philosophical Analysis*, an anthology of constructivist essayists that includes Peter Moore, Frederick Streng, Ninian Smart, and Robert Gimello (with whom—full disclosure—I took a class while an M.Div. student at Harvard Divinity School).

To understand, in a clear and succinct model, how the Katzean constuctivist argument works in an instance of contemporary scholarship, see for example Karen Jolly's essay "Father God and Mother Earth," included in *The Medieval World of Nature: A Book of Essays*. In a section of her essay entitled "Ways of Knowing: Mysticism," Jolly states that "mysticism" is simply a construct, a convenient device "used to cluster together a group of individuals, based on their records, who seem to have had a similar experience, and we then call these collective experiences a phenomenon, labeled mysticism." She states that specific expressions of mysticism are "framed within the individual mystic's worldview" and are a product of "his or her own cultural environment." (For this reason, she adds, it becomes difficult to locate treatises written by European mystics before 1100, because prior to that date the emerging scientific worldview had not split the "natural" world from the "supernatural." During the Middle Ages of the twelfth through fourteenth centuries, however, such mystical treatises abound.) Because mystical expressions are historically determined, Jolly contends, and because mystics are "inextricably intertwined with their own culture," it is impossible to develop a "universal or generic definition of mysticism as a basis of study." To do so "assumes that all 'mystics' in all religions have had the same essential experience but just describe it differently, according to their own religious traditions." Jolly therefore imposes two "rules" for discussing mysticism: "First, mysticism must be seen in its historical context. If a generic mysticism exists, it is an outsider's construct, useful only for comparison purposes because it can help focus discussion." Her second rule is, "what constitutes mysticism must be *defined* only by and within the historical context. To do otherwise...is to invoke parameters foreign to that culture."[1]

For incisive criticism of the Katz constructivist position that Jolly exemplifies so adroitly, I recommend Robert K. C. Forman's essay "Mysticism, Constructivism, and Forgetting," which comprises his introduction to *The Problem of Pure Consciousness: Mysticism and Philosophy*. This anthology, edited by Forman, includes monographs critiquing Katz and his supporters. I also recommend, in the same volume, Donald Rothberg's "Contemporary Epistemology and the Study of Mysticism." Forman frames the essential questions in the debate as these: "Has it been conclusively established" by the constructivists "that mysticism, indeed, is like most other experiences in the sense that it results from a process of introducing, imposing, or entertaining one's beliefs, expectations, judgments, and categories?" Or, on the contrary, "are there some experiences, or some specifiable aspects of human experience"—including the mystic's experience of pure consciousness—"that are not 'constructed' by our language and belief?"[2] Rothberg frames the questions as follows: "Is there a core mystical experience, a universal experience common to humans across cultures and traditions?" And, "Do mystical experiences give veridical insights into certain aspects of reality and into reality as a whole such that mystical claims should be accepted?"[3]

The collective answer that emerges from individual essayists in *The Problem of Pure Consciousness*—including Christopher Chapple, Paul J. Griffiths, Steven Bernhardt, Philip Almond, R.l. Franklin, Anthony N. Perovich, Jr., and others—is that while mystical experiences do of course differ between cultures, the perception of pure consciousness, common to these experiences and well-documented, is genuine and universal.

While I respect the sincerity and the intentions of Katz and his supporters, including Jolly, I have adopted a "middle path" between their constructivist attitudes regarding mysticism and the perennialist approach. In the present study I do locate the mysticism of Francis, Dōgen, and Rūmī within specific historical and cultural contexts: the thirteenth century of Christian northern Italy in the Holy Roman Empire, of Buddhist/Shinto Japan, and of Islamic Sufi society in Anatolia, a Persian culture ruled by the Mongol empire. But I propose that, despite these unique cultural and historical determinants, mystical realizations of Francis, Dōgen, and Rūmī—and indeed of people worldwide, throughout the centuries—share a common ground in direct experience of pure conscious awareness, fostered by the abnegation of ego. When articulated, this perennial human experience of a selfless, pure consciousness is, of course, constructed through distinct cultural symbols and specific languages for "the Sacred" and "the Absolute": union with God, disintegration of self into Allah, realization of original Buddha-nature, oneness with Brahma, communion with the Great Spirit, and so on. But the ground is universal.

Thus, without wishing to engage in the dualistic mind-trap of perennialist versus constructivist in the academic controversy, I note nevertheless that my position does place me in much closer sympathy with Forman's group than with Katz's.

*   *   *

Also, on another topic pertinent to discussions of mysticism, it is worth noting that Michel Foucault, in *The Hermeneutics of the Subject*, contrasts philosophy with spirituality, and discerns three characteristics of the latter in the West: first, spirituality "postulates that the truth is never given to the subject by right...by a simple act of knowledge.... for the subject to have right of access to the truth he must be changed, transformed, shifted, and become...other than himself." Second, "this conversion, the transformation of the subject...may take place in the form of a movement that removes the subject from his current status and condition (either an ascending movement of the subject himself, or else a movement by which the truth comes to him and enlightens him….let us call this movement, in either of its directions, *eros* (love). Another major form through which the subject can and must transform himself…is…a progressive transformation of the self by the self for which one takes responsibility in a long labor of *ascesis* (askesis)." Third, "spirituality postulates that once access to the truth has really been opened up…truth enlightens the subject; the truth gives beatitude to the subject; the truth gives the subject tranquility of the soul."[4] Thus Foucault emphasizes spirituality as a transformative praxis with consequences that reshape the being of the subject. With the great exception of the Gnosis, as he concedes, we can say that Foucault's description of Western spirituality stresses direct *experience* of the sacred, rather than knowledge of it, and thus is essentially a mystical one. In this light, Foucault restores a degree of mystical spirituality not only to such obvious candidates as Pythagoras and Plato, but also to the Stoics, Cynics, Epicureans, and Neo-Platonists,[5] Dōgen, Francis, or Rūmī would find interesting companions there.

Notes

Introduction: Three Mystics for Our Time

1. D.H.S. Nicholson, *Mysticism of Saint Francis*, 170.

2. Ursula King, *Christian Mystics*, 72.

3. John Daido Loori, "Dogen's 300 Koans and the Kana Shobogenzo," 52-63; Carl Bielefeldt, "Forum: Understanding Dogen," 30-39, 85-86.

4. Leslie Wines, *Rumi: A Spiritual Biography*, 13-14.

5. Bernard McGinn, *Presence of God, Vol. III*, 54; J. Thomas Rimer, ed., *Multiple Meanings*, 43; Annemarie Schimmel, *Triumphal Sun*, 35.

6. William Blake, "Auguries of Innocence," *The Portable Blake*, 150.

7. William Wordsworth, "The World is Too Much With Us," *The Norton Anthology*, 257.

Chapter One: Who They Were

1. Donald Spoto, *Reluctant Saint*, 4, 18, 22-26.

2. Steven Heine, *A Blade of Grass*, 28; Hee-Jin Kim, *Eihei Dōgen*, 18; Kazuaki Tanahashi in Dōgen, *Treasury of the True Dharma Eye*, xxxv.

3. Heine, *ibid.*, 27; Kim, *ibid.;* Tanahashi, *ibid.*, xxxv.

4. Spoto, *Reluctant Saint*, 34-35, 53-54; Adrian House, *Francis of Assisi*, 49.

5. Kim, *Eihei Dōgen* , 16; Tanahashi in Dōgen, *Treasury of True Dharma Eye* xxxiv; Etō Sokuō, *Zen Master Dōgen*, 96-104.

6. Hans-Werner Goetz, *Life in the Middle Ages*, 11-19.

7. Kenneth Clark, *Civilisation*, 62-66, 80; *30,000 Years of Art*, 575, 578-579, 583, 588, 591, 593, 597-598, 600-601.

8. Spoto, *Reluctant Saint*, 38; House, *Francis of Assisi*, 52.

9. John Haywood, *Historical Atlas*, 3.09, 3.17; House, *Francis of Assisi*, 90

10. Joyce E. Salisbury, *Medieval World of Nature*, 114-117.

11. Helaine Selin, *Mathematics Across Cultures*, 9.

12. Thomas Aquinas, *Aquinas Reader*, 39.

13. James J. Walsh, *Thirteenth: Greatest*, 166-177; Haywood, *Historical Atlas*, 3.08.

14. *The Mongol Conquests: Time Frame AD 1200-1300.*

15. Spoto, *Reluctant Saint*, 44; House, *Francis of Assisi*, 64, 68-70.

16. Kim, *Eihei Dōgen*, 19.

17. Dōgen, *Zen Poetry of Dōgen*, 75.

18. Peter Matthiessen, *Nine-Headed Dragon River*, 161; Sukuō, *Zen Master Dōgen*, 233.

19. Spoto, *Reluctant Saint*, 53-54; House, *Francis of Assisi*, 69-70.

20. Spoto, *Reluctant Saint*, 57-60; House, *Francis of Assisi*, 74-77.

21. William C. Chittick, *Sufi Path*, 1; Anne-Marie Schimmel, *Triumphal Sun*, 13.

22. Leslie Wines, *Rumi*, 23-31.

23. Peter Matthiessen, *Nine-Headed Dragon River*, 162; Kim, *Eihei Dōgen*, 20-21.

24. Dōgen, *Zen Poetry of Dōgen*, 97.

25. Valerie Martin, *Salvation*, 188; Spoto, *Reluctant Saint*, 122-128; House, *Francis of Assisi*, 129-141.

26. Francis, *The Little Flowers of St. Francis*, 63; House, *Francis of Assisi*, 120.

27. House, *Francis of Assisi*, 80, 82-83, 120; Spoto, *Reluctant Saint*, 69-70, 73-78.

28. House, *ibid.*, 80.

29. House, *ibid.*, 143; Spoto, *ibid.*, 138-142.

30. House, *ibid.*, 110,144-145, 152; Spoto, *ibid.*, 98, 117-118; Thomas of Celano, *Saint Francis*, 277-279; 498-499; Cunningham, *Brother Francis*, xiv, xxii; Nicholson, *Mysticism of Saint Francis*, 92.

31.Roberts, *History of World*, 299; *Mongol Conquests*, 9, 13, 18-19; Wines, *Rumi*, 31.

32. *Divine Campaigns*, 35; Desmond Stewart, *Early Islam*, 84; 90-97.

33. Rūmī, *The Soul of Rumi*, 325.

34. Wines, *Rumi*, 31, 174; 47-48, 174.

35. House, *Francis of Assisi*, 201-217; Spoto, *Reluctant Saint*, 155-168.

36. House, *ibid.*, 223-226; Spoto, *ibid.*, 170-173.

37. Kim, *Eihei Dōgen*, 24-25; Matthiessen, *Nine-Headed Dragon River*, 163-164, 175; Sokuō, *Zen Master Dōgen* , 177-212, 254-266.

38. Dogen, *Moon in a Dewdrop* 5; Dogen, *Treasury of True Dharma Eye*, xxxvi; Matthiessen, *ibid.*, 164.

39. *Moon in a Dewdrop*, 59-60; *Treasury of True Dharma Eye*, xxxvii; Kim, *Eihei Dōgen*, 27; Matthiessen, *Nine-Headed Dragon River*, 164-165; Sokuō, *Zen Master Dōgen*, 281.

40. Robert L. Thorp and Richard Ellis Vinogrand, *Chinese Art and Culture*, 227-229, 232, 234, 242, 260-261; "Song Dynasty in China: The Song Scroll": http://afe.easia.columbia.edu/song-scroll/song.html

41. Richard Stone, "Divining Angkor," 26-55.

42. Alvin M. Josephy, Jr., *500 Nations*, 43, 54, 62-65, 86; *30,000 Years of Art*, 568, 581.

43. Werner Gillon, *A Short History of African Art* , 90-92, 184-205, 341-346; Basil Davidson, *African Kingdoms*, 82-84, 131-141, 147; *30,000 Years of Art*, 592-594.

44. Moshe Idel and Mortimer Oslow, *Jewish Mystical Leaders*, 127-154; *Mongol Conquests*, 78.

45. Roberts, *History of World*, 298, 301; *Mongol Conquests*, 59.

46. Roberts, *ibid.*, 301; Haywood, *Historical Atlas*, 3.03.

47. Roberts, *ibid.*, 303, 363-364; Spoto, *Reluctant Saint*, 99; Edwin Bayrd, *Kyoto:* 67-68.

48. Lucille Schulberg, *Historic India*, 156-157.

49. Wines, *Rumi*, 55; Chittick, *Sufi Path*, 2.

50. House, *Francis of Assisi*, 256-263; Spoto, *Reluctant Saint*, 187-198.

51. McGinn, *Presence of God*, 75-87, 113; Furlong, *Visions and Longings*, 104-116, 148; Ursula King, *Christian Mystics*, 79, 88-99; Meister Eckhart: *Meister Eckhart*, xix-xx; House, *Francis of Assisi*, 87.

52. *Mongol Conquests*, 120; Amador Vega, *Ramon Llull*, 6, 259-261; Harvey J. Hames, *Art of Conversion:* 2; Huston Smith in *Essential Kabbalah*,, 12-13; Idel and Ostow, *Jewish Mystical Leaders*, 2-9, 15, 74; David Van Biema, "Found in Translation," 64.

53. Dōgen, *Treasury of True Dharma Eye*, xxxvii-xxxix; Kim, *Eihei Dōgen*, 31-38; Matthiessen, *Nine-Headed Dragon River*, 165-166; Sukuo, 288-305.

54. Francis, *The Little Flowers of St. Francis* 317.

55. House, *Francis of Assisi*, 273.

56. ibid., 276.

57. *ibid.*, 273-284; Spoto, *Reluctant Saint*, 200-210.

58. Dōgen, *Moon in a Dewdrop*, 7; Sokuō, *Zen Master Dōgen*, 565.

59. Sokuō, *ibid.*, 307; Matthiessen, *Nine-Headed Dragon River*, 172-178; Kim, *Eihei Dōgen*, 38-47.

60. Matthiessen, *ibid.*, 169; Dōgen, *Zen Poetry of Dōgen*, 123-124.

61. Dōgen, *Treasury of True Dharma Eye*, 3.

62. Dōgen, *Zen Poetry of Dōgen*, 123-124.

63. *ibid.*, cover illustration.

64. Wines, *Rumi*, 60-61.

65. Jean-Louis Michon, *xxi-xxv*, William C. Chittick, "Sufism and Islam," 21-32; Eric Geoffroy, "Approaching Sufism," 49-61; Rene Guenon, "Haqiqa and Shari'a in Islam,"89-100; Michon and Gaetani, *Sufism: Love & Wisdom*.

66. Wines, *Rumi*, 176; Chittick, *Sufi Path*, 2.

67. Kim, *Eihei Dōgen*, 39-44; Dōgen, *Treasury of True Dharma Eye*, xli.

68. Dōgen, *Zen Poetry of Dōgen*, 123-124.

69. Kim, 47.

70. ibid., 47-49; Matthiessen, *Nine-Headed Dragon River*, 186.

71. Dōgen, *Zen Poetry of Dōgen*, 99.

72. Chittick, *Sufi Path*, 3.

73. Schimmel, *Triumphal Sun*, 18.

74. Rūmī, 209-210.

75. Chittick, *Sufi Path*, 3; Schimmel, *Triumphal Sun*, 20.

76. Chittick, *ibid.*,, 241, 245; Shimmel, *ibid.*, 20.

77. Dōgen, *Zen Poetry of Dōgen*, 79-82, 8; Kim, *Eihei Dōgen*, 47.

78. Schimmel, *Triumphal Sun*, 23.

79. Matthisessen, *Nine-Headed Dragon River*, 195.

80. Kim, *Eihei Dōgen*, 49; Dōgen, *Zen Poetry of Dōgen*, ed. Heine, 94.

81. Dōgen, *Moon in a Dewdrop*, 219.

82. Schimmel, *Triumphal Sun*, 25-33.

83. Rūmī, *Soul of Rumi*, 7.

Chapter Two: Speaking to Us Across Centuries

※·※·※·※·※·※·※·※·※·※·※·※·※·※·※·※

Love

1. Lawrence S. Cunningham, *Saint Francis,* 59-60, 81; Clark, *Civilisation.* 74-76; D. H. S. Nicholson, *Mysticism of St. Francis,* 227, 244; Donald Spoto, *Reluctant Saint,* 211.

2. Cunningham, *Saint Francis,* 78-81.

3. Spoto, *Reluctant Saint,* 97; Lawrence Cunningham, ed., *Brother Francis,* xi-xii; St. Bonaventure, *Major Life of St. Francis,* 644.

4. Bernard McGinn, *Presence of God, vol. III,* 33.

5. Nicholson, *Mysticism of St. Francis,* 101; Friedrich Heer, "Saint Francis," 17; Cunningham, *Saint Francis,* 124.

6. Heer, "Saint Francis," 13.

7. Pope Francis, *Encyclical Letter* Laudato Si, 9.

8. Spoto, *Reluctant Saint,* 153; Cunningham, *Brother Francis,* 238; Adrian House, *Francis of Assisi,* 238.

9. Cunningham, *Saint Francis,* 30-31.

10. William M. Bodiford, *Sōtō Zen in Medieval Japan,* 28.

11. Dōgen, "Guidelines," *Moon in Dewdrop,* 35; "Bodhisttva's," ibid., 45; Hee-Jin Kim, *Eihei Dōgen,* 209. Dōgen, *Treasury of True Dharma Eye,* 475.

12. Dōgen, *Moon in Dewdrop,* 65.

13. William C. Chittick, *Sufi Path,* 194. See Anne-Marie Schimmel, *Triumphal Sun,* 332.

14. Chittick, *Sufi Path,* 187-191.

15. *ibid.,* 187 (emphasis added in line, "*He is totally empty…*").

16. *ibid.,* 197.

17. Eric Geoffroy, "Approaching Sufism," 55, St. John of the Cross, 17.

18. Chittick, *Sufi Path*, 73.

19. *ibid.*, 298.

20. *ibid.*, 339-340.

21. McGinn, *Presence of God, vol. III*, 41.

22. Chittick, *Sufi Path*, 333.

23. Schimmel, *Triumphal Sun*, 31.

24. Evelyn Underhill, *Mysticism*, 389.

Nature

25. Pope Francis, *Encyclical Letter* Laudato Si, 9.

26. Kenneth Clark, *Civilisation*, 61; Veronica Fraser, "Goddess Natura," 129-130.

27. Cunningham, *Brother Francis*, 147.

28. Thomas of Celano, "The First Life of St. Francis," 495-500, 1348.

29. Francis, in Habig, ed., *St. Francis: Writings, Early Bios.*, 134.

30. Lynn White, Jr., "Historical Roots of Our Ecological Crisis," 93.

31. Pope Francis, *Encyclical Letter* Laudato Si, 9-10. See Edward A. Armstrong, *Saint Francis: Nature Mystic*, 23, 238.

32. Dōgen, *Zen Poetry of Dōgen*, 31; *Treasury of True Dharma Eye*, 162.

33. Heine in Dōgen, *Zen Poetry of Dogen*, 31-32.

34. Kim, *Eihei Dōgen*, 210.

35. *ibid.*, 196; Heine in Dōgen, *Zen Poetry of Dōgen*, 31.

36. Kim, *Eihei Dōgen*, 197; Dōgen, *Treasury of True Dharma Eye*, 555.

37. Dōgen, *Treasury of True Dharma Eye*, 250. Variant in Kim, 129-130.

38. Kim, *ibid.*, 198-199.

39. *ibid.*, 199-200.

40. Dogen, *Zen Poetry of Dōgen*, 31.

41. Kim, *Eihei Dōgen*, 199-200.

42. Lucien Stryk in Basho, *On Love and Barley*, 16.

43. Chittick, *Sufi Path*, 19, 47-48, 51, 74. See Geoffrey, "Approaching Sufism," 58.

44. Schimmel, *Triumphal Sun*, 62, 75, 80, 83, 93-98.

The Body

45. Spoto, *Reluctant Saint*, 64.

46. Nicholson, *Mysticism of St. Francis*, 210-211.

47. Kim, *Eihei Dōgen*, 101.

48. *ibid.*, 100-104.

49. *ibid.*, 104. Variant translation: Dogen, *Treasury of True Dharma Eye*, 30.

50. *ibid.,* 101.

51. Chittick, *Sufi Path*, 43, 61-62, 74.

52. *ibid.*, 28-29.

53. *ibid.*, 28.

54. Schimmel, *Triumphal Sun*, 28; Chittick, *Sufi Path*, 29.

55. Chittick, *ibid.*, 301-302.

The Role of Women

56. Hans-Werner Goetz, *Life in Middle Ages*, 30, 40-43; Monica Furlong, *Visionings*, 18.

57. Goetz, *ibid.*, 40; J. M. Roberts, *History of World*, 415.

58. Spoto, *Reluctant Saint*, 124; McGinn, *Presence of God, vol. III*, 47.

59. McGinn, *ibid.*, 47.

60. *ibid.*, 48.

61. Dōgen, *Treasury of True Dharma Eye*, 81. Variant translation in Kim, 44.

62. Paula Kane Robinson Arai, "Women and Dōgen," 40.

63. Dōgen, *Treasury of True Dharma Eye*, 16.

64. Arai, "Women and Dōgen," 40-41.

65. Dōgen, *Treasury of True Dharma Eye*, 76, 80.

66. Dōgen, *Treasury of True Dharma Eye*, 79. Variant translation in Kim, 44.

67. Chittick, *Sufi Path*, 165-167, 181, 201.

68. *ibid.*, 168.

69. *ibid.*, 164.

70. Maria Massi Dakake, "'Walking Upon the Path of God Like Men'?": 133-134.

71. Schimmel, *Triumphal Sun*, 32; Dakake, *ibid.*, 138, 140-151; Wines, *Rumi*, 63-64, 68.

Spiritual Retreat and Social Engagement

72. Dakake, "Walking upon the Path," 144, fn.19; Titus Burckhardt, "Sufi Doctrine," 12.

73. Schimmel, *Triumphal Sun*, 28, 30-36.

74. Nicholson, *Mysticism of St. Francis*, 95.

75. *ibid.*, 300; Goetz, *Life in Middle Ages*, 64-65; 74.

76. Paul Sabatier, "Saint Francis," 27; Spoto, *Reluctant Saint*, 99.

77. Kim *Eihei Dōgen*, 42.

78. *ibid.*, 178.

79. *ibid.*, 43, 179.

Chapter Three: The Poetic Works

1. Dōgen, *Moon in Dewdrop*, 23; Kim, *Eihei Dōgen*, 3-4; Rūmī, *The Soul of Rumi*, 5.

2. McGinn, *Presence of God, vol. III*, 54-55.

3. Cunningham, *Saint Francis*, 58-59.

4. *Encyclical Letter* Laudato Si, 3.

5. *Presence of God* , *vol. III*, 55-56.

6. Fatemeh Keshavarz, *Reading Mystical Lyric*, 2.

7. Dōgen, *Zen Poetry of Dōgen,* trans. Heine, 7-8.

8. Wines, *Rumi*, 110.

9. Rumi, *Mystical Poems of Rūmī*, 13.

10. Rumi, *Mystical Poems of Rūmī 2*, 38.

11. *Zen Poetry of Dōgen*, 29.

12. *ibid.,* 110.

13. Rumi, *The Essential Rumi*, 166.

14. Rūmī, *Mystical Poems*, 5.

15. Schimmel, *Triumphal Sun*, 43.

16. Rūmī, *Essential Rumi*, trans. Barks, 253.

17. Keshavarz, *Reading Mystical Lyric*, 54.

18. *ibid.*, 50-71.

19. *The Kristeva Reader*, 95.

20. Dōgen, *Zen Poetry of Dōgen*, 10.

21. *ibid,* 103.

22. Dōgen, *Treasury of True Dharma Eye*, 449.

23. Kim, *Eihei Dōgen*, 81-88; Dōgen, *ibid.*, 534-536.

24. *Reading Mystical Lyric*, 20.

25. *ibid.*, 88-89.

26. *ibid.*, 89.

27. Dōgen, *Zen Poetry of Dōgen*, 40.

28. *ibid.*, 40-41.

29. Keshavarz, *Reading Mystical Lyric*, 37.

30. Dōgen, *Zen Poetry of Dōgen*, 36-37.

31. *Reading Mystical Lyric*, 37.

32. Dōgen, *Zen Poetry of Dōgen*, 36-37.

33. Rūmī, *Unseen Rain*, 28, 69; Rūmī, *Mystical Poems 2*, trans. Arberry, 37, 48, 72, 99; Keshavarz, *Reading Mystical Lyric*, 72.

34. Keshavarz, *ibid.*, 72.

35. Dōgen, *Zen Poetry of Dōgen*, 116.

36. *ibid.*, 37, 95, 109, 119, 126, 127.

37. Dōgen, *Moon in Dewdrop*, 218.

38. *ibid.*, 12. See also Kim, *Eihei Dōgen*, 200-201.

39. Cunningham, *Saint Francis*, 46.

40. Heine, *A Blade of Grass*, 7.

41. Dōgen, *Zen Poetry of Dōgen*, 112.

42. *ibid.*, 108.

43. Dōgen, *Moon in Dewdrop*, 219.

44. Rūmī, *Mystical Poems*, 11.

45. *ibid.*, 15.

46. *ibid.*

47. *ibid.*, 18.

48. Keshavarz, *Reading Mystical Lyric*, 41.

Chapter Four: What Francis, Dōgen, and Rūmī Offer Spiritual Seekers Today

1. See note 67, Chapter Two.

2. Kim, *Eihei Dōgen*, 101.

3. McGinn, *Presence of God, vol. I*, xv-xvi.

4. Sheldrake, *Spaces for the Sacred*, 122.

5. Merton, *Mystics and Zen Masters*, 6, 138.

6. Hadot, *Philosophy as a Way of Life*, 264-276.

7. Eliade, *Sacred and Profane*, 10-11 and *passim.*

8. Ricoeur, *Figuring the Sacred*, 48-55.

9. James, *Varieties of Religious Experience*, 299-300; Underhill, *Mysticism*, 81.

10. James, *ibid.*

11. Hadot, *Philosophy as a Way of Life*, 207-208; Arnold I. Davidson, 123-148.

12. James, 300.

13. *ibid.*, 299-300.

14. *ibid.*

Appendix: Some Further Considerations Regarding Mysticism

1. Jolly, "Father God and Mother Earth," 227-229.

2. Forman, "Mysticism, Constructivism, and Forgetting," 5.

3. Rothberg, "Contemporary Epistemology and Study of Mysticism," 164-165.

4. Foucault, *Hermeneutics of the Subject*, 15-16.

5. *ibid.*, 17.

Bibliography

Abe, Masao. *A Study of Dōgen: His Philosophy and Religion*. Ed. Steven Heine. Albany: State University of New York Press, 1992.

Ahmed, Shemsu-'D-Din. *Legends of the Sufis: Selected Anecdotes*. Trans. James W. Redhouse. London: The Theosophical Publishing House, 1976.

Allen, Paul M. and Joan deRis Allen. *Francis of Assisi's Canticle of the Creatures: A Modern Spiritual Path*. New York: Continuum, 1996.

Aquinas, Thomas. *An Aquinas Reader: Selections from the Writings of Thomas Aquinas*. Ed. Mary T. Clark. Garden City, NY: Image Books-Doubleday, 1972.

Arai, Paula Kane Robinson. "Women and Dogen: Teachings and Practices on Equality." *Mountain Record: The Zen Practitioner's Journal*. Fall 2002: 40-45.

Armstrong, Edward A. *Saint Francis: Nature Mystic*. Berkeley: University of California Press, 1973.

Barber, David. "Rumi Nation." *Parnassus: Poetry in Review* Vol. 25, Nos. 1 & 2: 176-209.

Basho. *On Love and Barley: Haiku of Basho*. Trans. and ed. Lucien Stryk. London: Penguin Group, 1988.

Bayrd, Edwin. *Kyoto: Japan's Ancient Capital*. New York: Newsweek Book Division, 1981.

Bielefeldt, Carl. "Forum: Understanding Dogen." *Buddhadharma: The Practitioner's Quarterly* Summer 2004: 30-39; 85-86.

Blake, William. *The Portable Blake*. New York: Viking Press, 1972.

Bodiford, William M. *Sōtō Zen in Medieval Japan*. Honolulu: Kuroda Institute-University of Hawaii Press, 1993.

Bonaventure. *The Soul's Journey into God / The Tree of Life / The Life of St. Francis*. Trans. Ignatius Brady. New York: Paulist Press, 1978.

Brunn, Emilie Zum and Georgette Epiney-Burgard. *Women Mystics in Medieval Europe*. New York: Paragon House, 1989.

Butler, Judith. *Gender Trouble: Feminism and the Subversion of Identity*. New York: Routledge, 1990.

Chittick, William C., trans. and ed. *Faith and Practice of Islam: Three Thirteenth Century Sufi Texts*. Albany: State University of New York Press, 1992.

Chittick, William C. *The Sufi Path of Love: The Spiritual Teachings of Rumi*. Albany: State University of New York Press, 1983.

Clark, Kenneth. *Civilisation*. New York: Harper & Row, 1969.

Cunningham, Lawrence, ed. *Brother Francis: An Anthology of Writings By and About St. Francis of Assisi*. New York: Harper & Row, 1972.

Cunningham, Lawrence S. *Saint Francis of Assisi*. Boston: Twayne Publishers-G. K. Hall, 1976.

Dakake, Maria Massi. "'Walking Upon the Path of God Like Men'? Women and the Feminine in the Islamic Mystical Tradition." *Sufism: Love & Wisdom*, ed. Jean-Louis Michon and Roger Gaetani. Bloomington, IN: World Wisdom, 2006.

Davidson, Arnold I., "Ethics as Ascetics: Foucault, the History of Ethics, and Ancient Thought," *The Cambridge Companion to Foucault*, second edition, ed. Gary Gutting. New York: Cambridge University Press: 2005.

Davidson, Basil. *African Kingdoms*. New York: Time-Life Books, 1974.

The Divine Campaigns: Time Frame AD 1100-1200. Alexandria, VA: Time-Life Books, 1988.

Dōgen. *Dōgen's Extensive Record: A Translation of the Eihei Kōroku.* Trans. Taigen Dan Leighton & Shohaku Okumara. Boston: Wisdom Publications, 2010.

Dōgen. *Flowers of Emptiness: Selections from Dōgen's Shōbōgenzō (Studies in Asian Thought and Religion, Vol 2).* Trans. Hee-Jin Kim. Lewiston, NY: Edwin Mellen Press, 1985.

Dōgen. *The Heart of Dōgen's Shōbōgenzō.* Trans. Norman Waddell & Masao Abe. Albany: State University of New York Press, 2002.

Dogen. *Master Dogen's Shobogenzo, Books 1-4.* Trans. Gudo Nishijima and Chodo Cross. Dogen Sangha, 2006.

Dōgen. *Moon in a Dewdrop: Writings of Zen Master Dōgen.* Ed. Kazuaki Tanahashi. New York: North Point Press-Farrar, Straus and Giroux, 1985.

Dōgen. *Shōbōgenzō: Zen Essays by Dōgen.* Trans. Thomas Cleary. Honolulu: University of Hawaii Press, 1986.

Dōgen. *The Shobo-Genzo.* Trans. Yuho Yukoi. Tokyo: Sankibo Buddhist Bookstore, 1986.

Dogen. *Sounds of Valley Streams: Enlightenment in Dogen's Zen. Translation of Nine Essays from Shōbogenzō.* Trans. Francis H. Cook. Albany: State University of New York Press, 1989.

Dogen. *Treasury of the True Dharma Eye: Zen Master Dogen's Shobo Genzo.* Ed. Kazuaki Tanahashi. Boston & London: Shambhala, 2012.

Dōgen. *The Zen Poetry of Dōgen: Verses from the Mountain of Eternal Peace.* Ed. Steven Heine. Boston: Tuttle Publishing, 1997.

Eliade, Mircea. *The Sacred and the Profane: The Nature of Religion.* Trans. Willard R. Trask. Orlando: Harvest/Harcourt, 1987.

Elverskog, Johan. *Buddhism and Islam on the Silk Road.* Philadelphia: University of Pennsylvania Press, 2010.

The Essential Kabbalah, ed. Daniel C. Matt. New York: Quality Paperback Book Club, 1998.

Forman, Robert K.C. "Mysticism, Constructivism, and Forgetting," *The Problem of Pure Consciousness: Mysticism and Philosophy,* ed. Robert K.C. Forman. New York: Oxford University Press, 1990.

Forman, Robert K.C., ed. *The Problem of Pure Consciousness: Mysticism and Philosophy*. New York: Oxford University Press, 1990.

Foster, Nelson, and Jack Shoemaker, ed. *The Roaring Stream: A New Zen Reader*. Hopewell, NJ: Ecco Press, 1996.

Foucault, Michel. *The Care of the Self*. New York: Pantheon, 1986.

Foucault, Michel. *The Hermeneutics of the Subject: Lectures at the College de France, 1981-1982*. New York: Picador, 2001.

Francis of Assisi. *Francis and Clare: The Complete Works*. Trans. Regis J. Armstrong & Ignatius C. Brady. Mahwah, NJ: Paulist Press, 1986.

Francis of Assisi. *Saint Francis of Assisi: Writings and Early Biographies*. Chicago: Franciscan Herald Press, 1973.

Francis of Assisi. *The Little Flowers of St. Francis*. Trans. Raphael Brown. Garden City, NJ: Image Books / Doubleday, 1958.

Fraser, Veronica. "The Goddess Natura in the Occitan Lyric." *The Medieval World of Nature: A Book of Essays*, ed. Joyce E. Salisbury. New York: Garland, 1993.

Fremantle, Anne. *Age of Faith*. New York: Time Incorporated, 1965.

Freke, Timothy. *Zen Wisdom: Daily Teachings from the Zen Masters*. New York: Sterling Publishing, 1997.

Furlong, Monica. *Visions & Longings: Medieval Women Mystics*. Boston: Shambhala, 1996.

Geoffroy, Eric. "Approaching Sufism." *Sufism: Love & Wisdom*, ed. Jean-Louis Michon and Roger Gaetani. Bloomington, IN: World Wisdom, 2006.

Gillon, Werner. *A Short History of African Art*. London: Penguin Books, 1991.

Goetz, Hans-Werner. *Life in the Middle Ages: From the Seventh to the Thirteenth Century*. Trans. Albert Wimmer, ed. Steven Rowan. Notre Dame: University of Notre Dame Press, 1993.

Gutting, Gary, ed. *The Cambridge Companion to Foucault*, second edition. New York: Cambridge University Press, 2005.

Habig, Marion A., ed. *St. Francis of Assisi: Writings and Early Biographies*. Chicago: Franciscan Herald Press, 1973.

Hadot, Pierre. *Philosophy as a Way of Life: Spiritual Exercises from Socrates to Foucault*. Ed. Arnold I. Davidson, trans. Michael Chase. Malden, MA: Blackwell Publishing, 1995.

Hames, Harvey J. *The Art of Conversion: Christianity and Kabbalah in the Thirteenth Century*. Leiden: Brill, 2000.

Haywood, John. *Historical Atlas of the Medieval World: AD 600 – 1492*. New York: Barnes & Noble Books, 2000.

Heer, Friedrich. "Saint Francis: The Medieval Man and His Culture." *Brother Francis: An Anthology of Writings By and About St. Francis of Assisi*, ed. Lawrence Cunningham. New York: Harper & Row, 1972.

Heine, Steven. *A Blade of Grass: Japanese Poetry and Aesthetics in Dogen Zen*. New York: Peter Lang Publishing, 1989.

House, Adrian. *Francis of Assisi: A Revolutionary Life*. Mahwah, NJ: HiddenSpring, 2001.

Huxley, Aldous. *The Perennial Philosophy*. New York: Harper & Row/ Colophon, 1970.

Idel, Moshe & Mortimer Ostow. *Jewish Mystical Leaders and Leadership in the 13th Century*. Northvale, NJ: Jason Aronson, 1998.

James, William. *The Varieties of Religious Experience*. New York: Touchstone-Simon & Shuster, 1997.

Jolly, Karen. "Father God and Mother Earth," *The Medieval World of Nature: A Book of Essays,* ed. Joyce Salisbury. New York: Garland, 1993.

Josephy, Alvin M., Jr. *500 Nations: An Illustrated History of North American Indians*. New York: Alfred A. Knopf, 1994.

Katz, Steven T., ed. *Mysticism and Philosophical Analysis*. New York: Oxford University Press, 1978.

Keene, Donald. *Japanese Literature: An Introduction for Western Readers*. New York: Grove Press, 1955.

Keshavarz, Fatemeh. *Reading Mystical Lyric: The Case of Jalāl al-Dīn Rumi.* Columbia, SC: University of South Carolina Press, 1998.

King, Ursula. *Christian Mystics: Their Lives and Leagacies Throughout the Ages.* Mahwah, NJ: HiddenSpring, 2001.

Kim, Hee-Jin. *Eihei Dōgen: Mystical Realist.* Boston: Wisdom Publications, 2004.

Kristeva, Julia. *The Kristeva Reader.* Ed. Toril Moi. New York: Columbia University Press, 1986.

Lane, George. *Early Mongol Rule in Thirteenth Century Iran: A Persian Renaissance.* London: RoutledgeCurzon, 2003.

Leidy, Denise. "A Thai Interpretation of Buddha Shakyamuni." *Buddhadharma: The Practitioner's Quarterly* Fall 2009: 70-71.

Leonard, Jonathan Norton. *Ancient America.* New York: Time Incorporated, 1967.

Lindholm, Charles. *The Islamic Middle East: Tradition and Change,* revised edition. Malden, MA: Blackwell Publishing, 2002.

Loori, John Daido. "Dogen's 300 Koans and the Kana Shobogenzo." *Mountain Record: The Zen Practitioner's Journal* Fall 2002: 52-63.

Loori, John Daido. *The Eight Gates of Zen: Spiritual Training in an American Zen Monastery.* Mt. Tremper, NY: Dharma Communications, 1992.

Martin, Valerie. *Salvation: Scenes from the Life of St. Francis.* New York: Alfred A. Knopf, 2001.

Matthiessen, Peter. *Nine-Headed Dragon River: Zen Journals.* Boston: Shambhala, 1998.

McGinn, Bernard. *The Presence of God: A History of Western Christian Mysticism. Vol. I-III,* New York: Crossroad, 1992-1998.

Meister Eckhart. *Meister Eckhart, from Whom God Hid Nothing: Sermons, Writings & Sayings.* Ed. David O' Neal. Boston: Shambhala, 1996.

Merton, Thomas. *Mystics and Zen Masters.* New York: Farrar, Straus and Giroux, 1967.

Michon, Jean-Louis and Roger Gaetaini, ed. *Sufism: Love & Wisdom.* Bloomington, IN: World Wisdom, 2006.

The Mongol Conquests: Time Frame AD 1200-1300. Alexandria, VA: Time-Life Books, 1989.

Nicholson, D. H. S. *The Mysticism of St. Francis of Assisi.* London: Jonathan Cape, 1923.

Nijō. *The Confessions of Lady Nijō.* Trans. Karen Brazell. Stanford: Stanford University Press, 1973.

The Norton Anthology of Poetry: Shorter Edition (New York: W. W. Norton & Company, 1970).

Pope Francis. *Encyclical Letter Laudato Si of the Holy Father Francis on Care for Our Common Home.* Rome: Vatican Press, 2015.

Reischauer, Edwin O. *The Japanese.* Cambridge, MA: Belknap Press, 1978.

Ricoeur, Paul. *Figuring the Sacred: Religion, Narrative, and Imagination*, trans. David Pellauer, ed. Mark I. Wallace. Minneapolis: Fortress Press, 1995.

Rimer, J. Thomas, ed. *Multiple Meanings: The Written Word in Japan – Past, Present, and Future. A Selection of Papers on Japanese Language and Culture and Their Translation Presented at the Library of Congress.* Washington, DC: Asian Division, Center for the Book, Library of Congress, 1986.

Roberts, J.M. *History of the World.* New York: Oxford University Press, 1993.

Rohr, Richard. *Eager to Love: The Alternative Way of Francis of Assisi.* Cincinnati: Franciscan media, 2016.

Rothberg, Donald. "Contemporary Epistemology and the Study of Mysticism," *The Problem of Pure Consciousness: Mysticism and Philosophy*, ed. Robert K.C. Forman. New York: Oxford University Press, 1990.

Rumi. *Daylight: A Daybook of Spiritual Guidance.* Trans. Camille & Kabir Helminski. Putney, VT: Threshold Books, 1990.

Rumi. *The Essential Rumi.* Trans. Coleman Barks. New York: Quality Paperback Book Club-HarperSanFrancisco, 1998.

Rumi. *Mystical Poems of Rumi*. Trans. A.J. Arberry. Chicago: University of Chicago Press, 1974.

Rumi. *Mystical Poems of Rumi 2*. Trans. A.J. Arberry. Ed. Ehsan Yarshater. Chicago: University of Chicago Press, 1991.

Rumi. *The Soul of Rumi: A New Collection of Ecstatic Poems*. Trans. Coleman Barks. New York: HarperSanFrancisco-HarperCollins, 2002.

Rumi. *Unseen Rain: Quatrains of Rumi*. Trans. John Moyne & Coleman Barks. Boston: Shambhala, 2001.

Russell, Bertrand. *A History of Western Philosophy*. New York: Simon and Schuster, 1945.

Sabatier, Paul. "Saint Francis as Religious Revolutionary." *Brother Francis: An Anthology of Writings By and About St.Francis of Assisi*. ed. Lawrence Cunningham. New York: Harper & Row, 1972.

Salisbury, Joyce E., ed. *The Medieval World of Nature: A Book of Essays*. New York: Garland, 1993.

Saunders, J.J. *A History of Medieval Islam*. London: Routledge, 2001.

Schimmel, Annemarie. *The Triumphal Sun: A Study of the Works of Jalāloddin Rumi*, second edition. London: East-West Publications, 1980.

Schulberg, Lucille. *Historic India*. New York: Time-Life Books, 1968.

Sedgwick, Henry Dwight. *Italy in the Thirteenth Century*. Boston, Houghton Mifflin: 1912.

Selin, Helaine, ed. *Mathematics Across Cultures: The History of Non-Western Mathematics*. Dordrecht: Kluwer Academic Publishers, 2000.

Sheldrake, Philip. *Spaces for the Sacred: Place, Memory and Identity*. Baltimore: Johns Hopkins, 2001.

Smith, Huston. *The World's Religions: Our Great Wisdom Traditions*. New York: HarperSanFrancisco-HarperCollins, 1991.

Smith, Margaret. *The Way of the Mystics: The Early Christian Mystics and the Rise of the Sufis*. London: Sheldon Press, 1976.

Smoley, Richard. *Inner Christianity: A Guide to the Esoteric Tradition*. Boston: Shambhala, 2002.

Sokuō, Etō. *Zen Master Dōgen as Founding Patriarch*. Trans. Ichimura Shohei. Washington, D.C.: North American Institute of Zen and Buddhist Studies, 2001.

"Song Dynasty in China: The Song Scroll." http://afe.easia.columbia.edu/song-scroll/song.html

Spoto, Donald. *Reluctant Saint: The Life of Francis of Assisi*. New York: Penguin Compass, 2002.

St. Bonaventure. "The Major Life of St. Francis." *St. Francis of Assisi: Writings and Early Biographies*, ed. Marion A. Habig. Chicago: Franciscan Herald Press, 1973.

St. John of the Cross. *The Dark Night of the Soul*. Trans. Gabriela Cunninghame Graham. New York: Barnes & Noble Books, 2005.

Stewart, Desmond. *Early Islam*. New York: Time Incorporated, 1967.

Stone, Richard. "Divining Angkor." *National Geographic* July 2009: 26-55.

Tanahashi, Kazuaki and Tensho David Schneider, ed. *Essential Zen*. Edison, NJ: Castle Books, 1996.

30,000 Years of Art: The Story of Human Creativity Across Time and Space. London, New York: Phaidon Press, 2007.

Thomas of Celano. *St. Francis of Assisi*. Trans. Placid Herman. Chicago: Franciscan Herald Press, 1963.

Thomas of Celano, "The First Life of St. Francis." *St. Francis of Assisi: Writings and Early Biographies*, ed. Marion A. Habig. Chicago: Franciscan Herald Press, 1973.

Thorp, Robert L., and Richard Ellis Vinograd. *Chinese Art & Culture*. Upper Saddle River, NJ: Prentice Hall, 2001.

Underhill, Evelyn. *Mysticism: A Study in the Nature and Development of Man's Spiritual Consciousness*, fourteenth edition. London: Methuen, 1942.

Van Biema, David. "Found in Translation: An English version of the Zohar, a guiding text of Jewish mysticism, offers new insights." *Time* 19 April 2004: 64.

Vega, Amador. *Ramon Llull and the Secret of Life*. Trans. James W. Heisig. New York: Crossroad, 2003.

Walsh, James J. *The Thirteenth: Greatest of Centuries*, twelfth edition. New York, Fordham University Press, 1952.

White, Jr., Lynn. "The Historical Roots of Our Ecological Crisis." *Brother Francis: An Anthology of Writings By and About St. Francis of Assisi*, ed. Lawrence Cunningham. New York: Harper & Row, 1972.

Wines, Leslie. *Rumi: A Spiritual Biography*. New York: Crossroad, 2000.

Acknowledgments

I am grateful to the scholars whose writings are cited in the bibliography and whose work has made mine possible. I am grateful also to Dr. Janina Safran and Dr. Charles Prebish, who advised me on this project in its earliest stages when it was my honors thesis at Penn State University, and to Dr. Anne Monius at Harvard Divinity School, who read it and offered invaluable advice and encouragement as I developed it further while a student in the Master of Divinity program there.

And to all my Ch'an and Zen teachers and all my spiritual mentors and fellow mystics—including Dōgen, Francis, and Rūmī—108 full bows.

I am grateful as well to my Zen students and my Spiritual Guidance students and clients, who teach me so much.

I also thank Paul Cohen at Monkfish Book Publishing Company for bringing this book into the world, and Colin Rolfe at Monkfish for layout work, Ginger Price for marketing, and everyone on the team there.

My deep appreciation to the small circle of intimate friends who sustain me, and to my loving family, to whom this book is dedicated. I take special note of my wonderful mother, Janet Ruhl, who proudly kept a manuscript of this book displayed on her living room coffee table for fourteen years, and who died two months before it was accepted for publication.

Printed in the USA
CPSIA information can be obtained
at www.ICGtesting.com
JSHW082208140824
68134JS00014B/492